TRACING YOUR TANK ANCESTORS

If you want to find out about the career of a soldier who served in tanks, are researching medals awarded to a tank crew member or just want to know more about a particular regiment, squadron or operation, this book will point you in the right direction.

Assuming that the reader has little prior knowledge of the history of British armoured forces, Janice Tait and David Fletcher trace their development from their formation during the First World War, through the Second World War and on to their role as an essential part of the British Army of the present day. Most important, they demonstrate how you can explore this history for yourself. They describe the records that are available and show how they can help you to reconstruct the career of a soldier who served in tanks or was connected with them. They also describe the kind of work the soldiers did, the armoured vehicles they worked with, and the men and women they served alongside.

This accessible, information-packed introduction to the history of British armoured forces will be essential reading and reference for anyone who is researching this aspect of military history.

Janice Tait is the librarian at the Tank Museum, responsible for the archive. Having a keen interest in family history research, Janice handles the many family history enquiries that arrive in the archive almost on a daily basis.

David Fletcher is the historian at the Tank Museum. He is one of the foremost experts on the history of British tanks and armoured vehicles. Among his many books are *The British Tanks 1915–19*, *Tanks and Trenches: First Hand Accounts of Tank Warfare in the First World War* and a series of studies of the key tanks of the two world wars.

LD 4310398 7

FAMILY HISTORY FROM PEN & SWORD

TRACING YOUR TANK ANCESTORS

A Guide for Family Historians

Janice Tait and David Fletcher

Published in association with the Tank Museum

THE TANK MUSEUM

Pen & Sword
FAMILY HISTORY

First published in Great Britain in 2011 by
PEN & SWORD FAMILY HISTORY
an imprint of
Pen & Sword Books Ltd
47 Church Street
Barnsley
South Yorkshire
S70 2AS

Copyright © The Tank Museum, 2011

ISBN 978 1 84884 264 9

The right of the Tank Museum to be identified as Authors of this Work
has been asserted by them in accordance with the Copyright,
Designs and Patents Act 1988.

A CIP catalogue record for this book is
available from the British Library.

Typeset in Palatino and Optima by
CHIC MEDIA LTD

Printed and bound in England by
CPI UK

Pen & Sword Books Ltd incorporates the imprints of
Pen & Sword Aviation, Pen & Sword Family History,
Pen & Sword Maritime, Pen & Sword Military, Pen & Sword Discovery,
Wharncliffe Local History, Wharncliffe True Crime,
Wharncliffe Transport, Pen & Sword Select, Pen & Sword
Military Classics, Leo Cooper, The Praetorian Press, Remember When,
ontline Publishing

ord titles please contact
OOKS LTD
orkshire, S70 2AS, England
nd-sword.co.uk
l-sword.co.uk

CONTENTS

INTRODUCTION

My father was in the Tank Corps: a statement that injects a certain amount of nervous caution into the hearts of people such as Janice and I when we deal with family history enquiries at the Tank Museum. You see, to us the Tank Corps is a very particular thing, covering a very specific period, from the summer of 1917 until October 1923. Before the earlier date it did not exist and even the word 'tank', in the context that we use it, held little meaning for most people. After the second date the correct title was the Royal Tank Corps, and from April 1939 the Royal Tank Regiment and it is by those dates that we define what we are talking about. However, to most people this would appear to be irrelevant detail.

In fact it is worse than that, as we have learned. Many enquirers use the term Tank Corps to mean any regiment that went to war in tanks at almost any time, be they cavalry, yeomanry or infantry and indeed, upon investigation, one has found that in some cases the person involved was a member of the Royal Artillery or the Royal Engineers or even the Royal Marines. They all served in tanks, or things that looked like tanks, but they were not members of the Royal Armoured Corps and beyond a few general suggestions we are unable to help. These distinctions are lost on most people but if we were to say that it is a bit like going into Waitrose to return something you had bought in Tesco you might have some idea.

To be more specific here are two common examples. Of the First World War we are often told by an enquirer that their ancestor went into action in the very first tank. For the record this was the Mark I male tank D1, commanded by Captain H. Mortimore, supported by Sergeant Davis, driven by Private Wateredge of the Army Service Corps while the rest of the crew comprised gunners Doodson, Leat, Hobson, Smith and Day. Eight men and we can name them all, but if you believe every enquirer that tank must have been packed to the gills, worse than the Northern Line in the rush hour. That is the trouble with family history: it relies too much on hearsay. Or we are told, of the Second World War 'he' was one of the Desert Rats, which in popular terminology is shorthand for 'he served in North Africa'. You see the Desert Rats were, specifically, members of the 7th Armoured Division whose divisional sign, painted on their vehicles and sewn onto their tunics was a stylised jerboa (*Jaculus Orientalis*) in bright red. Even if we can confirm this the matter is by no means at an end. The 7th Armoured Division in its heyday comprised six tank regiments and one armoured car regiment of the Royal Armoured Corps along with infantry, engineers, artillery and all manner of other branches of the army, all of whom wore the divisional shoulder flash, all of whom were entitled to call themselves Desert Rats but, as far as we are concerned, only those men who served in the armoured regiments, in tanks or armoured cars, qualify.

The last British soldier to take part in the Great War died as we started work on this book and another link was lost. He was over 100 – he would have to have been – and this emphasises the distance we have come since that time, but even the Second World War is also drifting into history; many who participated in that conflict are now over 80. What this means is that familiarity with the terminology of that time is slipping from the national consciousness. When one uses terms such as division, brigade, regiment or battalion these days it is necessary to explain them because they are meaningless to the majority of people.

It would be a lot easier if the British Army could be treated as a whole, but it cannot. Its history is glamorous, confusing, fascinating and frustrating by turns and it harks back for centuries. Nobody can expect to know it all and in any case the army doesn't work like that. The many corps see themselves as an entity in their own right, with their own history, customs, traditions and idiosyncrasies. Sometimes you get the impression that as far as they are concerned the rest of the army does not exist. And if anything the fighting regiments, in particular those of the Infantry and the Royal Armoured Corps are even worse. It has been said, and rightly, that in the British Army a man's regiment is his family: where he feels at home, where his mates are – it is that regiment, and particularly those mates, that he is fighting for. This is not easy for a civilian to understand but it is something we need to be aware of if we are to have any hope of making any sense of what is going on. The regiment, in the British

Army, is almost a sacred thing and that is why it features largely in these pages.

Ask an American veteran who he served with and he will name a division; the Screaming Eagles, Hell on Wheels, the Ozarks and so on, but a British veteran will name his regiment. There are exceptions: men who served in a corps, such as the Royal Signals, Royal Electrical and Mechanical Engineers or the Royal Army Service Corps for example – large organisations which served all British divisions – will often name that division as theirs, or a regiment if appropriate. However, it is worth bearing in mind that locating their records will depend upon the cap badge they wore, not the formation that they were attached to.

And there is another matter to be considered. A regiment might move from one brigade to another, or the brigade be transferred from one division to another or indeed a regiment be lifted out of its brigade and its division and inserted somewhere else altogether. Such procedures are so common, so involved and so complicated that a book such as this is simply not big enough to cope and the best way to follow examples like that is by consulting Orders of Battle.

It can get even worse than that, although thankfully not on a large scale. There is at least one instance during the Normandy campaign when one regiment was so badly mauled by the enemy, and its numbers so reduced, that it was amalgamated with a brother regiment that was in somewhat better shape. Temporary amalgamations had occurred earlier, when numbers were severely depleted but in those instances the regiments were reborn and reinstated. If amalgamation was not possible, or for any reason a regiment was deemed surplus to requirements it could be summarily disbanded. In no time at all the survivors would find themselves posted to other regiments, often so swiftly that their feet hardly touched the ground.

Two examples also come to mind of regiments that, having been effectively wiped out, were recreated at the expense of other regiments, which, for all practical purposes, vanished off the face of the earth. Both the 4th and 7th battalions of the Royal Tank Regiment, having already lost all of their tanks, were ultimately captured when General Klopper surrendered the Tobruk garrison to Rommel on 20 June 1942.

Call it sentimentality, call it tradition, but there was a determination that these two battalions, which were high in the Royal Tank Regiment hierarchy and had fought alongside one another before, should not vanish for good. So 7th RTR was recreated in Britain in 1943 by the simple expedient of renaming 10th RTR, who simply had to rename their tanks and sew a different coloured patch onto their uniforms. As for 4th RTR, it had to wait until 1 March 1945 before it reappeared, by the somewhat more sensitive and complicated process of renaming another tank regiment which had no connection with the Royal Tank Regiment at all. This was 144th Regiment, Royal Armoured Corps, itself created from an infantry battalion, the 8th East Lancashire Regiment.

Yet there is a parallel case which is not so easy to explain. The 3rd Royal Tank Regiment was detached from 1st Armoured Division and sent, on Winston Churchill's insistence, to Calais where it landed on 22 June 1940 to find the port city already under threat from the Germans. The regiment might just as well have been thrown in the sea. Very few men came home, and none of the tanks, but the 3rd somehow managed to survive and ultimately went out to the Middle East with new men and new tanks, although if there was anyone left from the 1940 battalion it would have been very surprising.

The fact is that this is a complicated and involved subject and the most we can hope to do in these pages is to provide an outline. The first question we ask of anyone who comes to us with family history enquiries is: 'Which regiment was he in?' If we can establish that then we at least have something to start from. It is an unfortunate fact that unless the man in question was a senior officer, or won a gallantry award or was unfortunate enough to be killed in action then the chances are that we will never be able to do more than say that if he was a member of that regiment then he was probably doing whatever that regiment was doing on a given day, as recorded in the Regimental War Diary; but proving it, or being able to say what he as an individual was doing, is virtually impossible.

This book has been planned to work on two levels. On one, it is hoped, it provides a good outline history of the Royal Armoured Corps, its predecessors and its constituent parts. This should be useful to anyone with an interest in regimental history and tank history in particular, whether for the purpose of family research or general history. On the other level it offers guidance to anyone trying to research the military life and times of a family member by indicating the various sources available in the many and varied archives in the United Kingdom.

Do not imagine for a minute that it will be easy. Whatever you do please do not believe what you see on the television. Those programmes are fine as a source of inspiration but the researchers hired by the television company not only have huge resources at their disposal, they can also pick and choose the evidence they present and make the entire thing look easy. Your task could be expensive, time consuming and frustrating but if you persevere it can be immensely rewarding. You will undoubtedly learn a great deal and discover a new respect for your ancestor, no matter what you find out about him. But above and beyond that you will be adding something, no matter how small, to history and that in itself, is quite an achievement.

Resources Available for Tracing your Tank Ancestors

The Tank Museum is the regimental museum for the Royal Tank Regiment and its predecessors and the Corps Museum for the Royal Armoured Corps. Therefore many of the resources referred to in these chapters are from the Tank Museum's Archive and Reference Library, although there are many other resource centres mentioned, including online sites.

As with any form of family history research, tracing an ancestor who was in tanks is often quite difficult. If you have documents left by your ancestor, such as pay books and even travel documents and photographs, then this should be the place to begin and you will certainly have a head start.

The first step, however, for everyone should always be to try to acquire your ancestor's service record, although this can sometimes be problematical whether it is for the First World War or through to present-day records. Many of the First World War records held by The National Archives in London were damaged during the Blitz of the Second World War, although some survive and are known as the 'Burnt Records', so this is always the best first step to take and you may be lucky. After 1920 the service records are held at the Army Personnel Centre in Glasgow and because of data protection issues, you do have to be next of kin to apply for a copy of the record in the first twenty-five years after the date of death, although some basic information can still be obtained by those who are not next of kin. This will probably change over the next few years, when more of these records will be transferred to The National Archives, making them available to everyone.

The key information on these records is the regimental name or the battalion number for Tank Corps/Royal Tank Corps and Royal Armoured Corps Regiments. This will enable you to at least find information of where your ancestor served, even if he is not mentioned by name in any other document. A common enquiry is to find the route a relative took, particularly during the Second World War, as the family quite often want to visit the places where the soldier saw action. Sadly if your relative was killed during the Second World War, then it is probably easier to find information about him.

The first step then should always be to try to obtain a copy of his service record if possible. First World War service records can be searched at The National Archives in person at:

The National Archives
Ruskin Avenue
Kew
Surrey TW9 4DU
Tel: 0208 876 3444
www.nationalarchives.gov.uk

For post-1920 records a Service Access Request form (SAR) is initially required. There are a number of ways that this form can be acquired:

By post: Army Personnel Centre
Historic Disclosures, Mailpoint 400
Kentigern House
65 Brown Street
Glasgow G2 8EX
Email: disc4@apc.army.mod.uk
Tel: 0141 224 2742
www.veterans-uk.info/ or www.army.mod.uk

One thing to bear in mind when a service record is received is that army documents are often littered with abbreviations, which were obvious to the people at the time, but the meaning of which has now been somewhat lost. We will not be including a list of abbreviations in this book as this has been done in many other books, including the Imperial War Museum's *Tracing Your Family History: Army* and online at The National Archives. There is one exception, however, which is the entry on the service record indicating X and Y lists. Almost all army service records of the Second World War will include references to the X and Y lists, which have never been fully understood but probably refer to the following. The X list was used to record when men were absent from their regiment for more than twenty-one days. For example, if they were in hospital, missing, a prisoner of war or even a deserter. Initially, on return, they would not have necessarily returned to their own regiment but this was later changed and then they normally did return to their original unit. The Y List appears to be when a soldier was about to be demobbed or placed in the reserve.

Other useful sources include:

The Imperial War Museum (www.iwm.org.uk)
The Imperial War Museum in London records all aspects of the two world wars and other operations involving Britain and the Commonwealth since 1914. The records are particularly useful for looking for photographs of particular units or operations. They also hold an excellent collection of oral histories, including many tank-related recordings and personal papers of tank personnel.

Imperial War Museum
Lambeth Road
London SE1 6HZ

Commonwealth War Graves Commission (CWGC) (www.cwgc.org or tel: 01628 634221)
The CWGC supplies information on the location of graves and memorials worldwide. Information on the individual includes name, rank, service number, regiment, date of death, age, home town, place of death and next of kin.

Newspapers and Journals
The British Library newspaper archive (www.bl.uk) and other online newspaper archives hold most national newspapers and some specialist newspapers. Local reference libraries or record offices will hold copies of local newspapers, which often include details of soldiers who were killed, awarded gallantry medals or had other interesting stories to tell.

London Gazette (www.gazettes-online.co.uk)
Notification of honours and awards are listed, occasionally with a citation explaining why the award was granted. These may be published some time after the award was granted. Few citations were published during the Second World War.

Army Lists
Army lists give details of the careers of army officers and sets can be found at the Imperial War Museum and the National Army Museum. The Tank Museum holds an incomplete set.

War Memorials Trust (Email: info@warmemorials.org)
The Trust maintains war memorials in Great Britain, monitoring the condition of memorials and offering advice on conservation.

United Kingdom National Inventory of War Memorials
(www.ukniwm.org.uk)
This register is based at the Imperial War Museum and covers over

60,000 UK war memorials. At present the facility to search for names on the memorials is not possible but it is hoped that this will be available next year.

County Archives

County archives are usually run by the county council and so the relevant county council website will usually have a link to their archives. The archive will generally hold parish registers for births, marriages and deaths, census returns, electoral registers, etc. – particularly useful for tracing First World War ancestors is the 'absent voters' lists for 1918/1919. These will give the regiment and personal number of a soldier who survived the war.

Family History Societies

There are many family history societies across the country and a full list can be obtained from the Federation of Family History Societies (www.ffhs.org.uk); most have individual websites. There are also many regional FHS fairs held during the year, the largest probably being the 'Who Do You Think You Are?' show at Olympia in London. This show has a large military history component.

Prisoners of War Information

The National Archives has various documents relating to prisoners of war, including 'Prisoner of War Interviews and Reports' (WO161). Further documents are listed in Chapter 4.

There is not complete information online concerning prisoners of war, but the following organisations may help:

National Ex-Prisoner of War Association (www.prisonerofwar.org.uk)

British Army Prisoners of War 1939–1945 (www.ancestry.co.uk), which lists over 107,000 British Army prisoners of war, of all ranks, held in Germany and occupied territories. Each entry includes rank, POW number, regiment or corps, and camp location.

Far East Prisoners of War (www.cofepowdb.org.uk)

British Red Cross (www.redcross.org.uk)

The International Committee of the Red Cross (www.icrc.org)
Archives Division and Research Service
International Committee of the Red Cross
19 Avenue de la Paix
Geneva CH-1202, Switzerland

There is quite a hefty research fee for using this service.

Chapter 1

UNDER THE WHITE ENSIGN

The origin of the tank, indeed its very inspiration, is tied up so closely with the Admiralty, the Royal Naval Air Service and specifically Winston Churchill that it deserves an introductory chapter. The whole matter of armoured warfare on land, at least as far as Britain is concerned, is due to one officer, Commander Charles Rumney Samson, RN, who established his Eastchurch Squadron of the Royal Naval Air Service at Dunkirk and, in the first weeks of the war, on days when flying was not possible, waged a buccaneering sort of conflict against German forces in Flanders in motor cars.

Samson's Motor Bandits as they were called, and regarded by regular British forces in the area, were not exactly models of organisation. Car crews appear to have been chosen on a first come first served, every man for himself basis, only increasing as the number of vehicles increased or more volunteers turned up.

> Every now and then the Navy produces an officer who exactly suits an emergency for the very reason he has what may be termed a natural 'piratical' character. Of that type Samson was an excellent example . . .
>
> Having involved the Royal Naval Air Service in the land battle he found the Army was having trouble with the German Uhlan patrols, horse soldiers reminiscent of Waterloo days with long spears and a tendency to stick to main roads for raids. Samson, having another enthusiasm for fast cars, born from experience at Brooklands track, seized his opportunity and 'obtained' a number of suitable cars which he fitted with Maxims and gave the opposing cavalry hell.
>
> Recollections of S.C.H. Davis.

Order was ultimately imposed from above when Churchill, at the Admiralty, authorised the construction of sixty somewhat-improved armoured cars of a more or less standard pattern, organised into four fifteen-car squadrons, which were established under Samson from October 1914.

In time these things grew, as they will. A better design of armoured car began to appear in 1915, along with armoured gun lorries and motorcycle machine-gun combinations which, by April, had expanded into nine armoured car squadrons, each with a dozen armoured cars and three gun lorries, three squadrons of six gun lorries only and five squadrons of motorcycle machine-gun combinations, most of which could boast eighteen machines and supporting transport. This was established as the Royal Naval Armoured Car Division under Commander F.L.M. Boothby, RN, based, to begin with, in the *Daily Mail* airship sheds at Wormwood Scrubs; although matters relating to recruiting were handled by Royal Naval Air Service headquarters at the Crystal Palace.

REPORT on the ARMOURED CAR SQUADRONS of the
ROYAL NAVAL AIR SERVICE (AEROPLANE SUPPORT)

The men recruited for the Cars were largely Chauffeurs, Garage Mechanics and Scottish Engineers. They were recruited chiefly from London, Liverpool (through the Royal Automobile Club) Derby (through Rolls-Royce Ltd.) and Glasgow.

From this point matters started to deteriorate as far as the Royal Navy and armoured cars are concerned. As the trench lines on the Continent became established opportunities for mobile warfare decreased and many squadrons went further afield in search of action. Also around this time (April/May 1915) Winston Churchill left office as a result of the Dardanelles operation so the Armoured Car Division lost its most influential supporter and there is evidence of friction with the army in France. With a few exceptions these units were disbanded and their vehicles handed over to the War Office.

However, in the months before he left the Admiralty Churchill had initiated an entirely new concept of armoured warfare which was to grow beyond the most optimistic imaginings. In February 1915 he ordained the creation of an Admiralty Landships Committee under Eustace Tennyson d'Eyncourt and ten months later the first tank was born. By this time, of course, the army had taken over but in the meantime the Royal Navy had made preparations, in conjunction with Churchill's wishes while he was at the Admiralty.

> In the middle of January, 1915, talking the whole position over once more with Mr Churchill in his room at the Admiralty, he desired me to carry out the following experiment . . . Striding up and down his room, he outlined what was in his mind and drafted the following minute. Whilst doing this, at intervals, he would stop and say 'We must crush the trenches in D. A. D. We must crush them in. It is the only way. We must do it. We will crush them in. I am certain it can be done.'
>
> Commodore Murray Sueter, Director of Air Department

Churchill's experiment and the subject of the minute was his idea of using pairs of conventional steam rollers to crush in the trenches and flatten them out. Sueter tried it; it did not work. Subsequent experiments with tracked vehicles showed more promise and resulted, by the end of 1915, in the production of two famous prototypes, 'Little Willie' and 'Mother' – the world's first tanks.

The plan was to form four landship squadrons (Nos. 20 through 24) to provide the crews for the new machines; in fact, for the reasons given above, this never happened and only 20 Squadron was formed – it was charged with undertaking experimental work, in the course of which it had built up a great deal of experience. This is why, from 1915 until the end of the war, tanks in Britain – be they experimental ones or production machines en route to France – are seen with naval personnel in attendance not soldiers. Not only did the men of 20 Squadron continue with experimental work but they also took the responsibility of testing newly made tanks and then seeing that they were delivered to British ports for onward shipment to France.

Of course the ideal thing would have been to transfer these men to

On 30 June 1915 20 Squadron, Royal Naval Air Service laid on a demonstration of the progress they had made in designing a landship. A number of senior army officers attended along with David Lloyd George (far right) the minister of munitions and Winston Churchill (behind the large post) the ex-First Lord of the Admiralty. Thomas Hetherington, who at one and the same time seems to have been a cavalry officer and a flight commander in the RNAS, is driving the Killen-Strait tractor as it cuts through the barbed wire.

the army but that was one move they were entitled to reject if they did not want to. Colonel Ernest Swinton (great-uncle of the actress Tilda Swinton) who was then a leading light in the army's interest in landships hoped to persuade the navy men to transfer. This is his account of what happened at Bisley on 9 March 1916:

> To avoid confusion in the expected ugly rush of stalwart recruits I called the parade to attention as if hailing the main-top and rasped out
>
> 'Ratings wanting to transfer, one pace forward – march!'
>
> The front rank swayed, seemed to lean backwards – so rigid was it – and not a man moved! The explanation was simple.

These men were being paid by the Admiralty about three times the amount they would have received on transfer to the Army!

As a result 20 Squadron remained under the Admiralty, although for administrative purposes it transferred to the Royal Marines. Only one name appears to have survived from this time, a Chief Petty Officer Hill of 20 Squadron who is said to have driven the prototype tank 'Mother' at Hatfield Park in February 1916.

The Machine Gun Corps was formed on 14 October 1915, initially by removing the heavy Vickers-Maxim machine guns and their men from individual infantry battalions and grouping them together in their own battalions with a new cap badge of crossed machine guns and a new identity; the corps soon came to see itself as an elite force. It was probably the first time that the British Army had taken the machine gun seriously.

Even so there was a precedent. As early as November 1914 a Motor

Men and machines of the Motorcycle Machine Gun Corps on parade at Bisley Camp in Surrey. Cap badges, invariably hidden under goggles, would be Royal Artillery and later Machine Gun Corps.

This photograph is believed to show the very first tank men at Bisley with Lieutenant Colonel W.R. Bradley in the foreground. At this time they would be known as the Heavy Section, Machine Gun Corps and worn the MGC cap badge.

Machine Gun Service had been formed at Bisley, in Surrey, which employed motorcycle sidecar units mounting Vickers guns in order

to supply mobile firepower support to the infantry. These were, for some reason, administered by the Royal Artillery. Their role in fact was identical to that of the motorcycle machine-gun squadrons of the Royal Naval Armoured Car Division, which were there to provide similar support to the Royal Naval Division. Indeed it seems reasonable to assume that these Royal Naval units were organised along the same lines as the Motor Machine Gun Service, which had preceded them by about ten months.

What the navy called squadrons the army referred to as batteries, and although they were mounted on different machines the arrangement would appear to have been the same. A battery comprised three sections and a section consisted of two machine-gun-mounted sidecar units and four others which served to carry ammunition, additional manpower and, in the last resort, act as a replacement carrier for the gun. There were, in time, twenty-five of these batteries scattered around the world. They were absorbed into the Machine Gun Corps when that was formed and will come to our attention again quite soon.

Meanwhile there is another title to attract our attention: the Machine Gun Corps (Motors). This was coined in October 1915 and it embraced the Motor Machine Gun Service, mentioned above, most of the armoured cars taken over from the Royal Naval Armoured Car Division that summer and a few stray military units that found themselves, by some whim of fate, operating armoured vehicles. The armoured cars were organised as batteries (of four armoured cars each) but rejoiced in a variety of titles. There were Armoured Motor Batteries (AMB), Light Armoured Car Batteries (LACB) and Light Armoured Batteries (LAB) – joined, from 1916 onwards, by eight-car Light Armoured Motor Batteries – the famous LAMBs. Most of these units were ultimately absorbed into Tank Corps' armoured car companies after the war.

> *The Motor Cycle* obtained over 10,000 recruits voluntarily for the Army motor sections, including the famous TANKS. A letter of appreciation was subsequently received from the Army Council.
>
> *The Motor Cycle*, 8 March 1917

Beyond that these armoured car units do not concern us any further and are only mentioned here in order to complete the picture. In the same spirit it should be explained that there were many other more or less obscure armoured car units operating under War Office control but not necessarily as part of the Machine Gun Corps. There were, for example, at least sixteen Armoured Motor Batteries in India during the war, mostly manned by local personnel and as active as local enthusiasm might or might not make them.

From the Records of No. 1 Armoured Motor Unit – Captain A.J. Clifton:

> Unit formed at Peshawar, 26 July 1915 consisting of one officer, 20 men and 3 armoured motors (Rolls-Royce).
>
> After five weeks training it proceeded on Field Service – Mohmand Operations 1915. Three Minerva cars were added temporarily for these operations, at the conclusion of which it resumed its normal strength of three Rolls-Royce cars.
>
> Returning to Peshawar in December 1915 it was quartered there till September '16 when it again took the field against the Mohmands.

There were also the Light Car Patrols, operating in the Middle East in totally unarmoured Model T Fords some of which appear to have been absorbed into armoured car companies of the Tank Corps after the war, but we will come to them later.

The three Rolls-Royces of 1st Armoured Motor Unit in India. To begin with these men could have come from any regiment stationed out there, later they could be absorbed into the Machine Gun Corps.

By Major L.V. Owston D.S.O.
commanding Siwa Column
4th March 1917

ORDER OF MARCH
1. Light Ford Car Patrols.
2. Column Headquarters signal detachment.
3. Light Armoured Car Brigade.
4. Motor Transport column.
5. Repair Cars, Light Armoured Car Brigade.

Since it generates so much interest by association we might mention the Hedjaz Armoured Car Section which operated with Lawrence of Arabia. This was formed in May 1917 with two Rolls-Royce armoured cars which appear to have come from No. 10 (Royal Navy) Armoured Motor Battery. These were joined by two more cars from No. 1 Armoured Motor Battery in December and then by the remainder of that battery in June 1918, whereupon it was retitled the Hedjaz Armoured Car Battery until it was disbanded in October. It was joined, from November 1917, by No. 10 Motor Section, Royal Field Artillery which had a couple of ten-pounder guns carried portée fashion in Clement-Talbot light trucks (or tenders) of which it had six.

Finally, as an example of how men can be moved around by the rough and tumble of war, the following may serve. In October 1915 the Royal Navy created the Russian Armoured Car Division under Commander Oliver Locker-Lampson, MP, with Royal Naval Air Service personnel and thirty or more Lanchester armoured cars from 15 and 17 squadrons. They sailed for Russia in December 1915 and remained there for two years supporting the Czar's Imperial forces until the Bolshevik Revolution changed everything. They were administered by the Royal Marines from November 1917.

The men returned from Russia although their cars did not. However, soon after they arrived home these navy men were informed that they would now be transferred to the army, specifically the Machine Gun Corps, and were directed to the corps' headquarters in Grantham, Lincolnshire. By the end of January 1918 they set off, by a roundabout route, to Basra in Iraq. Here they waited until some armoured cars arrived: Austins this time, accompanied by Ford vans. Officially designated the Dunsterforce Armoured Car Brigade under Major General Lionel Dunsterville of the Indian Army, they were usually referred to almost telegraphically as 'Duncars'. Pushing up through north Persia into southern Russia with the objective of securing the Caspian oilfields from falling into Turkish hands they failed because the entire region was in a chaotic state. They withdrew and the force returned to Britain where it was disbanded in March 1919. However, we shall meet their cars again.

Some months after this, in another attempt to reach and dominate the same area North Persia Force (Norperforce) was created, which included 15th Light Armoured Motor Battery equipped with Rolls-Royce armoured cars. This managed to reach Enzeli, on the Caspian Sea, but the situation there, both tribal and political, was simply too unsettled to control and, although the retreat was less precipitate than that of Dunsterforce it was still a retreat, in ridiculously harsh conditions.

The following account of an armoured car action involving Norperforce is taken from an article by Captain M.A. Wilcox in the *Royal Tank Corps Journal*, Volume XV.

> Armoured cars played an important part from then onwards (19 May 1920 – the retreat from Enzeli) and were sent to patrol the road as far as Naglobar, 25 miles north of Menjil . . . On one of their first patrols the armoured cars captured a Bolshevik Ford car near Rustamabad, the occupants abandoning their car on the approach of the section. A few days later the cars, under Lieutenant H Wood, rounded a bend two miles north of Rustamabad and were heavily fired on by about 100 Bolsheviks on the hillside. The cars returned their fire until one car had its petrol tank punctured by a ricochet off the ground. The despatch rider pluckily connected the tow rope under fire, and Lieutenant Wood, with great presence of mind, withdrew the section . . .
>
> During the evacuation of Menjil the 15th L. A. M. B. had to

abandon one Rolls-Royce, due to a back axle breaking on the steep hill leading out of the village. Before leaving the car steps were taken to render it of no use to the enemy . . .

On October 26th the Bolsheviks were observed by the British to be in possession of Rustamabad, about 1.5 miles from the Jubin position. The armoured cars at this time were placed as follows:-

One section at Jubin, under Lieutenant McCabe.

One section at Menjil, under Lieutenant Wood and myself (Wilcox).

It was at once decided to carry out a reconnaissance against the Bolsheviks' position and the 122nd Rajputana Infantry, with one section of armoured cars, advanced on Rustamabad. Owing to Lieutenant McCabe being admitted to hospital, Sergeant Lievesley took the cars into action and met with heavy fire from machine guns concealed in the mud huts of the valley. After advancing to within 300 yards of the machine guns, where the road was blocked by a barricade, he withdrew the cars after covering the retirement of the Rajputanas. For his part in this action Sergeant Lievesley was awarded the Persian Order of Merit.

Resources

If you are lucky (or unlucky) enough to have ancestors who were involved in the development of armoured cars and tanks, then below are some sources which may be useful. Many of the previously mentioned quotes can be found in documents and books held at either the Tank Museum or The National Archives.

The National Archives (TNA)

Personal visit:

Royal Navy Commissioned Officers and Non-Commissioned Officers who entered service during or before 1924 (ADM 196)

No 20 Squadron Operations Record Book (AIR 27/258) plus other documents at AIR 1

Naval Medal Rolls (ADM 171) for campaign medals

Online:
www.documentsonline.nationalarchives.gov.uk for the Register of Seaman's Service (ADM 188) for RNAS ratings who served before 1918.

The Royal Naval Division ('Winston's Little Army') (ADM 339) includes many personal details, if the service record has survived.

Machine Gun Corps

There is no official museum for documents relating to the Machine Gun Corps, although Operational War Diaries and other official documents can be found at The National Archives, and the Tank Museum holds some documents relating to the Heavy Branch of the Machine Gun Corps. There is, however, an active Machine Gun Corps Old Comrades Association (www.machineguncorps.co.uk), which will answer email enquiries at info.mgc@ntlworld.com.

Documents at the Tank Museum Archive and Reference Library

Various documents relating to Royal Naval Air Service (RNAS) Armoured Car Squadrons, including S.C.H. Davis's 'Notes on Commander Samson' (E1976.9) and 'Men of the Machine Gun Corps 1915–1922' (TM E2009.3514) – this spreadsheet lists men by name, rank, number (including any former numbers), unit (including any former units), decorations, date of death and place of birth. The original *Machine Gun Corps Magazine 1918/1919* (TM E1991.32.4.5) is also available.

Books

Brooks, Richard and Little, Matthew, *Tracing your Royal Marine Ancestors*, (Pen & Sword, 2008, ISBN 978 1 84415869 0)
The marines have been involved with armoured vehicles from 1914 to the present day, so the above book may be useful for anyone tracing their ancestor who was in 'tanks' but not in the Royal Armoured Corps.

Tomaselli, Phil, *Tracing your Air Force Ancestors,* **(Pen & Sword, 2007, ISBN 978 1 84415 573 6)**

The Royal Naval Air Service was involved with armoured cars from 1914, eventually forming the Royal Navy Armoured Car Division. They were also used during the inter-war period and during the Second World War. Records for personnel are in various repositories, but Operation Record Books do survive and can be found in The National Archives and the Fleet Air Arm Museum.

Sueter, Rear Admiral Murray F., *Airmen of Noahs: Fair Play for our Airmen,* **(Sir Isaac Pitman & Sons, 1928)**

Swinton, Major General Sir Ernest, *Eyewitness,* **(Hodder & Stoughton, 1932)**

Fleet Air Arm Museum

Royal Naval Air Service
Yeovilton, Nr Ilchester
Somerset BA22 8HT
www.fleetairarm.com

Use of the research facilities is by appointment. The Fleet Air Arm Museum Archive hold sets of documents relating to service before and during the First World War, for Royal Naval Air Service and Royal Naval Division ratings and some officers.

Chapter 2

THE WAY IN

W here did these men come from, these pioneers who would take the first tanks into action across the pitted landscape of the Somme? The simple answer is 'everywhere' but we can suggest three main sources. Some came from civilian life because they had mechanical skills. Geoffrey Smith, editor of *The Motor Cycle* magazine appointed himself a sort of unofficial recruiting officer, drawing in men from the motor trade: 'It all started through my keen interest in motor cars and motor cycles which commenced in 1908, and my experience in this respect coupled with being a regular reader of *The Motor Cycle* . . .' (William Taylor Dawson, C Company).

Others came from the ranks of the Army Service Corps since, it was believed, they possessed the aptitude to drive these strange, new monsters. Many of these men came from the ASC Tractor Depot at Avonmouth Docks near Bristol where the work involved the turnaround and maintenance of Holt caterpillar tractors from the United States en route for France; the fact that they already had some experience of tracked vehicles may have played a part. They were all, ostensibly, volunteers who stepped forward on the understanding that the work they were being asked to do was of 'a secret nature which might prove dangerous'. Army Service Corps men also came in from the main recruiting depot in London while some even came from caterpillar companies already operating in France.

However, the majority of men came from the ranks of the Machine Gun Corps and, in particular, some 700 men of the Motor Machine Gun Service – then training at Bisley in Surrey under Lieutenant Colonel R.W. Bradley, who also transferred. Sites at Bisley particularly associated with these nascent tank men were Stickledown Range, the isolated Siberia Camp and Bullhousen, sometimes called Bull House

Farm (probably because it sounded less Teutonic). Here various ranges were earmarked, upon which the men could learn the intricacies of the Hotchkiss and Vickers machine guns and the heavier six-pounder (57mm) guns that would be fitted to the male tanks. These guns, however, could not be fired safely on what was, after all, a mere rifle range. Training was therefore limited to gun drill, without firing. In order to shoot, men were sent to the Royal Artillery range at Larkhill on Salisbury Plain and to HMS *Excellent* or HMS *Pembroke* the Royal Navy's gunnery schools at Whale Island in Portsmouth Harbour and Chatham respectively.

No. 711 Company, Army Service Corps, was formed in May 1916 to provide drivers for the first tanks. They retained ASC cap badges to begin with but note that the chap on the right in the rear rank has the word TANK emblazoned on his uniform.

Officers were also plucked from a variety of sources. Colonel Ernest Swinton, first commander of the new arm, which at this time was known simply as the Tank Detachment (the word 'tank' at that time having no military significance that anyone was aware of), managed to commission a number of cadets from the Machine Gun Corps Training Centre at Grantham, and from three battalions of the Royal Fusiliers (the Universities and Public Schools Brigade). Swinton visited Chelsea Barracks in addition to Oxford and Cambridge universities, seeking men with mechanical aptitude from an engineering background, but it appears that other qualities were also valued. Commanding officers of infantry battalions in Britain were asked to nominate suitable types and from the Royal East Kent Regiment (the 'Buffs') at Canterbury came Basil Henriques and George MacPherson. Interviewed by Swinton in London they could not muster between them enough knowledge of engines or guns but both were accepted anyway.

Our interview with Colonel Swinton was short. He told us that a profoundly secret new unit of the Machine-Gun Corps was being formed, but he gave us no hint as to its purpose.

'What do you know about motor-cars?' he asked.

'Nothing at all, sir' I replied.

'What machine-guns can you use?' was his next question.
I mentioned one, having just returned from a special course in musketry.

'That is the only one we don't use' he said 'Do you know the Lewis?'

The reply was in the negative.

George fared no better, except that he could drive a car.

The Colonel looked us up and down, again emphasised the utmost secrecy of what we were going to do, told us that we should learn more when we joined the unit, and after giving us our tickets to Bisley, dismissed us with these words.

'If you are no use, you will be sent back to Dover at the end of a fortnight.'

Sir Basil Henriques

As an example listed below are the officers selected to command the first six tank companies, along with their origins:

A Company, Major C.M. Tippets, The South Wales Borderers

B Company, Major T.R. McLellan, The Cameronians

C Company, Major A. Holford-Walker, The Argyll and Sutherland Highlanders

D Company, Major F. Summers, Royal Naval Air Service

E Company, Major N.H. Nutt, Royal Naval Air Service

F Company, Major W.F.R. Kyngdon, Royal Artillery

The unit title was changing too, faster than most people could keep track of it. The Tank Detachment gave way, in about April 1916, to the Armoured Car Section of the Motor Machine Gun Service, which may well have been considered a bit too literal, for in May 1916 it became the Heavy Section, Machine Gun Corps, which was adjusted to the Heavy Branch, Machine Gun Corps in November, though even that was not the end of it.

In June 1916, before these matters of organisation and command had been settled, a new site had been selected for tank training in Suffolk, just south of the Norfolk town of Thetford. Centred on Lord Iveagh's estate at Elveden, but incorporating land owned by Lord Cadogan and the Duke of Grafton, it was flat farmland which was used, in season, for shooting game birds. Now, however, it was totally depopulated on army orders, sealed off from public access by two cordons of sentries from the Home Defence Corps. Parts were converted into a convincing replica of the front line in France, with British and German trenches, an area of no man's land and appropriate strongpoints. This work was undertaken by men of the Royal Engineers under Major Giffard Le Quesne Martel; this same corps also supplied an officer, Colonel Solomon J. Solomon, to camouflage the machines, as well as wireless operators to try out new sets which might be used in tanks.

The organisation of a company – one that was complete for war – comprised four sections, each of six tanks, plus one spare tank in reserve – that is, twenty-five tanks in all. The company was commanded by a major, each section by a captain and each tank –

The crew of tank C14 Corunna *with their officer, Second Lieutenant F.J. Arnold. C14 took part in the first ever tank battle but became stuck in a shell hole and three of these men died.*

except for that commanded by the section commander – by a lieutenant or second lieutenant. The seven other men in each tank crew comprised a non-commissioned officer (NCO), five men usually classed as gunners and a driver, an Army Service Corps man who still retained his ASC cap badge.

In addition to the tank crews, say 175 men and 25 officers, each pair of companies would have what might be termed administrative staff. There would be a second-in-command of course, a couple of junior staff officers, a workshop officer, a sergeant major, a quartermaster sergeant and probably eighty or ninety more men. Swinton tells us that the Heavy Section had a total of eleven motor cars, twenty-seven motorcycles and ninety-nine bicycles but there must have been more. For example, another source tells us the Army Service Corps contingent also had thirteen box vans, three charabancs, fifteen 30cwt lorries and twenty-seven 3ton lorries, along with cars and motorcycles. They also had three 105hp Foster-Daimler tractors to tow and provide power for the workshop trailers.

The matter of Army Service Corps involvement at this stage probably warrants closer attention since, in addition to its historical significance, it highlights some of the hazards awaiting historians in general as well as those engaged upon family history research. We have to rely to a large extent on the evidence provided by Captain H.P.G. Steedman, ASC, who in 1916 was in charge of the vehicle park at Elveden, including inspection, maintenance and the training of tank drivers. At that time he was Second Lieutenant Steedman, serving under the senior ASC man, Major Hugh Knothe. Steedman was pursued for his recollections by the officer in charge of ASC records but his first submission seems to have gone astray and by the time they caught up with him again, in the summer of 1917, he was commanding an Army Service Corps company in Palestine. Under normal circumstances a year would not be a long time – in war it could be a lifetime and in Steedman's case this was compounded by the fact that he lost all of his papers when His Majesty's Transport *Arcadian* was torpedoed and sunk in the Aegean in April 1917 en route to Alexandria.

Steedman obviously survived but he lost all of his possessions and this traumatic experience, coupled with his own prejudices and hearsay must have had some influence on his recollections. We must, therefore, consider his evidence with care, seek corroboration where we can and evaluate what he says accordingly. This is not an isolated case, it is merely selected to illustrate that any length of time after an event, short or long, the words of an individual will be no more than a version of the truth, based upon that individual's perception. What we can say for sure is that by May 1916 a new unit, No. 711 Company, Army Service Corps, had been created for these men, initially under the command of Hugh Knothe with Second Lieutenant St John in charge of the mobile workshops. Steedman is very critical of the early tanks but not of the men; he says they 'worked harder and more willingly' than any he had ever met despite dreadful conditions 'loading and unloading (tanks) at all hours and in all weathers'. Some, apparently, found the new machines so intimidating that they pretended ignorance of mechanical matters and were returned to their original units in some disgrace. Steedman believed that with a bit more care and understanding their confidence could have been recovered and he points out that despite what they had been through these men never gave away the secrets of what they had seen.

Just to round off the story of the first six companies at this stage the history of F Company merely explains that it left Thetford (meaning Elveden) for Wool (meaning Bovington) on 27 October

Members of the crew of His Majesty's Landship War Baby *a Mark I female tank of the Gaza Detachment, Tank Corps in Palestine. The men belonged to E (5th) Battalion commanded by Major Norman Nutt.*

Tank crew and infantry cluster around Lieutenant Hastie's tank D17 Dinnaken *where it came to rest after the Flers battle. Notice the fancy camouflage pattern on the side of the tank. This was rarely seen after 1916.*

1916. E Company, by contrast, claims that it was formed at Bovington on 17 November 1916. It does not mention Elveden at all. However, this history is selective at best. The interesting thing is the immediate outcome of this. It had been agreed that a few tanks might be of some value to the Egyptian Expeditionary Force in their struggle against Turkish forces in the Middle East, north of the Suez Canal. According to Lieutenant Steedman eight Mark I tanks from Elveden, transported down to Bovington, were promptly earmarked for despatch to the Middle East along with a detachment of men of E Battalion (as it was now called). These eight tanks were hardly new: they had been used for training at Elveden and were probably fairly tired by then. This has resulted in claims that the tanks sent out to Egypt were wrecks, instead of more modern machines as promised, but at the time, December 1916, they were all that was available. The detachment, commanded by Major Norman Nutt, arrived in Alexandria on 9 January 1917 and subsequently took part in the Second Battle of Gaza in April 1917. It was the first time that tanks were to plant their tracks in this alien environment, but by no means the last.

The only tanks in existence at this time were the Mark I type, of which 150 were ultimately built. They weighed around twenty-eight tons and were a little over thirty-two feet long, including a wheeled tail that acted as a stabiliser and steering aid. The tanks were divided equally between male and female types. The former mounted a 57mm gun – usually referred to as a six-pounder – in a sponson on each side whereas the female machines had two heavy machine guns per side instead. Both types required a crew of eight, four of whom were involved, to some extent, with driving the tank while the other four manned the guns. The interior was hot, noisy and full of exhaust fumes and, since these early tanks had no springs at all, very uncomfortable. They were also painfully slow, with a top speed of about 3mph on good ground, but in 1916 they were the latest thing – top-secret, war-winning weapons which naturally attracted the best men.

Tanks went into action for the first time on 15 September 1916. Machines from both C Company (Major Allen Holford-Walker) and D Company (Major Frank Summers) made history and a modest contribution to the final throes of Douglas Haig's Somme offensive of 1916, just sufficient to ensure their survival. A Company was also in France at this time but not yet ready for action, while B, rather short of tanks, followed at the end of the month.

> Our tank commander was 2nd Lt Macpherson [commanding female tank C20], a fine and likeable young fellow, but he, like all of us had never been on an actual battlefield or in action before . . .
>
> We reached a point which we believed was our objective and after a while, as our petrol was getting low, we had to return some distance where we were joined by the other Tank of our section. Both it and ourselves came up against machine-

gun fire with armour-piercing bullets and whilst we had a few holes I counted upwards of 40 in the other Tank. Our success was perhaps only limited, due to the impossible ground and the fact that there were only 32 tanks spread over a front of about 7 miles or more . . .

Gunner W.T. Dawson, C Company

Owing to the mechanical condition of the tank in Flers (I expected the engine to pack up at any time) I eventually withdrew and struggled very slowly back up the Flers/ Delville Wood road for a short distance, when I left what was left of the road, turning left-handed and had just reached the edge of a hillock about 200 yards from the road when our engine packed up for good.

That was September 15th for me!

Lieutenant Stuart Hastie commanding D17 *Dinnaken*

The War Office issued a set of war establishments for the Heavy Branch, Machine Gun Corps on 18 November 1916. It lists all the staff at headquarters, also at the headquarters of what was shortly to become a tank battalion, of a workshop and a tank company of twenty tanks. It would be pointless to list them all in a work such as this but some are worth mentioning, just to give some idea of what a range of tasks there were for which men were required. Most would be Heavy Branch personnel although some, like staff car drivers, would be attached from the Army Service Corps.

The headquarters, for example, had five clerks, eight orderlies, four telephonists and six batmen, while the attached personnel included three drivers and an interpreter. The battalion headquarters did not have any telephonists, nor an interpreter, but it did have a cook and a surprisingly large number of attached personnel. There were two officers, one Royal Army Medical Corps, the other Army Service Corps, and an attached batman for each; one clerk but thirty-seven Army Service Corps drivers covering a fleet of vehicles. The workshops, as one might imagine, had many more specialists: blacksmiths, wheelers, electricians, coppersmiths and so on plus eight general fatiguemen and, rather oddly for such a mechanised unit, six drivers for pack animals. In the tank company itself, again as might be expected, the majority of individuals comprised the crew for twenty tanks but there is an interesting footnote to the effect that tank crews should include three drivers for each tank, presumably meaning that the first driver and gearsmen were interchangeable.

Haig was certainly impressed enough to demand more tanks, which was just as well since a continuation order for 1,000 machines had already been placed. At the rate of eight men per tank, never mind support and administrative staff, this meant a substantial increase in recruitment. It also required a considerable expansion of manufacturing capacity and, indeed, space for training.

To begin with tank production was shared between two companies; William Foster & Co. of Lincoln and the Oldbury Rail-

Meanwhile, back in Britain, men of 20 Squadron, Royal Naval Air Service, remained responsible for testing and delivery of production and prototype tanks such as this experimental petrol–electric example photographed in 1917.

way Carriage and Wagon Company in Staffordshire – although shared is probably not quite the right term. The Oldbury Company, which was part of Dudley Docker's Metropolitan Carriage Wagon and Finance Company, undertook to build 113 machines while Fosters were responsible for 37 tanks, some of which they attempted to hive off to their neighbours, Robey and Co., though this seems to have failed. There was also a problem, owing to the secrecy surrounding the tank project, in identifying the fact that workers were engaged upon valid war work and Albert Stern was obliged to use strong-arm tactics in order to obtain badges proving that they were so employed.

It should also be pointed out that many other firms were engaged in elements of tank construction: Daimler in Coventry, for instance, producing engines and gearboxes or steel producers such as William Beardmore and Co. in Glasgow, who provided armour plate. And there were examples of an exchange of roles between civilian workers and soldiers. In an effort to get sufficient numbers of tanks up and running to be sent to France staff were sent from Birmingham to Elveden to work alongside the tank men while tank men went to the factories in order to help the factory workers in building the tanks.

Meanwhile plans went ahead both in Britain and France to expand the tank force in terms of men as well as machines. The plan, which started to come into effect in October 1916, was to enlarge the exist-ing companies to the size of battalions, create three new battalions – making nine in all – and then group these, three at a time, into brigades. The means by which this was achieved is not well explained in surviving accounts and the picture is both complex and confusing. For example, A Company, which had been in France since September, records that it was split into three and moved to new locations in November – these three groups then forming the nucleus of the three companies that would form the new A Battalion. In Britain the situation seems to have been even more confusing.

A gunner who served with C Company, 8th Battalion and signed himself 'W.F.L.' wrote:

I was at Hounslow Barracks in the M. T. A. S. C. [Motor Transport Army Service Corps] when the rumour went around that a large percentage of that Corps was to be transferred into either the Infantry or the Tank Corps. At that time [1916] very little was known of Tanks, and naturally much speculation was rife among the troops (especially those who had no desire to go into the Infantry) as to what sort of a unit it was likely to be and the kind of work one would be called upon to perform.

Many will recollect the harrowing tales that were current in the barrack-room or canteen. Tanks, said some, gifted with vivid imaginations, were monsters to be avoided like the plague . . .

According to the history of E Battalion the centre of tank activity moved from Elveden to Bovington in Dorset on 27 October 1916. This can hardly have taken place overnight but whether the 27th marks the beginning or the completion of this process is not clear. The battalion history dates its creation from 17 November 1916 and gives its organisation as three companies, each of four sections and four tank crews per section plus a headquarters. It uses the term crews, rather than tanks, presumably because tanks were in very short supply at that time.

A typical battalion would have thirty-six tanks split between three companies of twelve tanks each. The companies were further sub-divided into sections but the arrangements appear to have been variable to suit the battalion. In some a company was split into three sections of four tanks each while others preferred four sections of three tanks. Taking all the attached personnel, such as Royal Army Medical Corps, armourers, fitters and so on, the total manpower of a fully staffed battalion would be 682, 674 of whom would be Tank Corps.

The preamble to F Battalion's history is both more detailed and more confusing. It states that the establishment at Elveden was divided in two. One half, known as the 'Training Centre' – which was responsible for weapons training and everything else that did not involve tank driving – became 2nd Battalion upon arrival at Bovington, while the other half, known as the 'Area' at Elveden was responsible for tank driving, and became 3rd Battalion. It goes on to say that battalions 1 to 5 were numbered so 'according to the positions they occupied in the camp'.

A published history of Bovington (*Bovington Tanks* by George and Anne Forty, Dorset Publishing Co., 1988) tells us that E and F battalions, along with headquarters, occupied an area to the west of the main road that runs through the camp while G, H and I battalions dwelled on the east side. The F Battalion history also paints a vivid picture of new recruits arriving at Bovington. It says that towards the end of November 1916 'men arrived in great numbers, fresh from their civilian occupations. Each day large numbers were marched up from Wool station and passed before the Medical Officers; those who were passed fit being taken in hand by the Quartermaster's Department and the rejected were sent back to their homes.'

Percy Jarvis experienced this: he came to Bovington in December 1916 and this is an extract from his first letter home: 'We have been medically examined and all but two of us passed so I expect we shall stay here now. We saw some of the tanks this morning and they are rather funny things . . .'

These men will have been those recruited under the Derby Scheme (a deferred voluntary enlistment scheme initiated by the Earl of Derby), who, unlike conscripts, appear to have had some choice in the matter of the arm of service they joined. The F Battalion history says that these men formed the main strength of its B and C companies while A Company had come down from Elveden and were from the Motor Machine Gun Service. The Derby Scheme men they described as 'keen . . . to take part in the most up-to-date method of fighting', which was tanks of course.

At the same time the companies in France, as they struggled to expand, found that many of their men were being recalled to Britain since they embodied all the practical experience there was in the technical and operational side of tank fighting. Most would be promoted and serve either as instructors at Bovington or as officers and NCOs of the new battalions.

Writing in 1919 Major Clough Williams-Ellis, MC, ('The Tank Corps', published by *Country Life*) says of the new recruits that, in addition to providing fighting tank crews and workshop personnel, each battalion included a 'curious collection of miscellaneous individuals, tailors, barbers, shoemakers and clerks' and that was only part of it. Williams-Ellis also remarks that the early success of the tanks and the ensuing publicity drew in men from every branch of the army but 'especially the infantry – [for whom] the ordinary battle routine – to put it conservatively – [had] begun to pall'.

Turning to the officers, he says, 'At first each individual wore the dress of his original unit, so that there was a strange collection of uniforms at Bermicourt – Scottish bonnets and kilts, riding breeches, and bandoleers, every conceivable dress, even to naval blue.' What this means of course is that apart from those who had come direct from civilian life virtually everyone had come from other parts of the armed forces, which could prove to be a significant part of an individual's story.

Bermicourt is a village near St Pol, on the northern side of the road from Montreuil to Arras, and the elegant chateau there became headquarters to the Heavy Branch and the Tank Corps as it became the following year. Here one found the new commander of the tanks in France, Colonel Hugh Elles and his staff, which included Captain G. Le Q. Martel as brigade major, Captain T.J. Uzielli as quarter-master, Captain J.H. Tapper as staff officer and Captain F.E. Hotblack the intelligence officer.

North-west of Bermicourt, along the winding valley of the river Ternoise, a huge complex of workshops, stores, tank parks and training grounds built up, centred on the villages of Teneur, Erin, Blangy, Rollancourt and others, which absorbed hundreds of tank men who were never affiliated to particular battalions. The organisation was set up in December 1916, under the command of Major J.G. Brockbank, Army Service Corps, who with a small staff struggled to come to terms with the requirements of an arm that was still in its infancy. Starting in January 1917 work began on erecting buildings on a site near the village of Erin which would become, in due course, Tank Corps Central Workshops.

Another nearby village, Wavrans, was selected as the site for the railhead and the original tank park, or Tankodrome as it was called then. Here railway sidings were installed but before they were ready tanks started to arrive: veterans from the Somme and new ones direct from England. The tanks were unloaded after dark by inexperienced personnel, in bitterly cold conditions. Tanks were then

Turn out the guard: a muddy scene at the entrance to Central Workshops at Erin. The men now have brass TC (Tank Corps) shoulder titles but note the figure, second from the far end in the front rank. In the Tank Corps this man was classed as a trumpeter, rather than a bugler.

issued to the newly created battalions and driven to their new homes nearby.

The typescript history of Central Workshops and Central Stores, carried through until the end of the war is a constant litany of overwork, difficulties of supply and cooperation from England and a recurring shortage of manpower. This was alleviated to some extent in the summer of 1917 by the arrival of three Chinese Labour Companies: the 51st, 69th and 90th, amounting in all to over 1,100 men. They undertook work of all kinds, appropriate to their skills, and in particular are credited with the manufacture of some 400 fascines and 110 tank sledges for use in the Battle of Cambrai – work done almost exclusively by Chinese personnel.

In the space available to us it is impossible to deal with everything but readers should be aware that various units span off from the Central Workshops and would also have absorbed Heavy Branch or Tank Corps personnel. These included salvage companies (later known as field companies) who scoured the battlefields to recover whole tanks or useful bits of them, battalion workshop companies (one attached to each battalion), which provided mechanical first aid to broken-down or damaged tanks, and the advanced workshops, equipped with mobile workshops that supported the above.

> During the first part of January, B. Batt. Workshops Coy. were engaged in putting as many tanks as possible into running order. The men were mostly of the Derby class and the majority of them were quite new to the work, though a few of them were from 711 Co. M. T. A. S. C. The officers also, with the exception of 2/Lt (now Major) Wenger, were equally new to tanks. But as all had had previous experience in their trade or profession, the work went on very well in spite of the somewhat scanty supply of spares and tools and the wet and muddy conditions.
>
> Major E.R. Parsons, MC

Meanwhile at Merlimont, on the Channel coast south of Boulogne the Heavy Branch established a gunnery school staffed by tank men, where crews were trained, retrained on new weapons and given refresher courses while taking advantage of the seaside to relax and get fit. Further south still at Le Trépot a large reinforcement camp was set up, while across the estuary, at Mers-les-Bains there was a medical facility and convalescent centre. Tank soldiers worked at all these locations, though they were not all in tanks by any means.

In the summer of 1917 Merlimont was also the site of a special experiment enacted under the code name 'Operation Hush'. This was a scheme to land an amphibious force, including nine tanks, on the Belgian coast to seal off Ostend. In the event it never took place, although the troops were well rehearsed, particularly in the matter of scaling the tricky sea wall using special devices that prefigured the Normandy Landings in 1944. A special tank detachment, probably formed from volunteers from all battalions, was commanded by Major the Hon. J.D.Y. Bingham of 8th (H) Battalion; they were kept virtually incommunicado from June until October 1917, when the scheme was abandoned. It only affects a few men but might explain gaps in some individuals' stories.

Back in Britain Bovington Camp expanded rapidly. In addition to a basic tank school, which today we would call a driving and maintenance school, it featured an intelligence school, a compass school, a gas school and a pigeon school, soon to be joined by a revolver school and workshops. In April 1917 land was acquired on the coast, east of Lulworth Cove, and a gunnery school was established where six-pounder guns and machine guns could be fired safely out to sea. Of course all of these establishments would have staff of their own, most of whom would be Heavy Branch (later Tank Corps) personnel.

It was the nature of these early tanks, their ponderous movements and vulnerability to wear and tear, which dictated their use. Virtually all movement was by rail so it was only worth using them en masse, in set-piece battles. You would not send two or three tanks out to do a job at short notice. Thus it is possible to list the battles and the tank battalions involved with a reasonable degree of accuracy.

In April 1917 sixty-two tanks, shared between what were now C and D battalions, were to support a big offensive near Arras, including Vimy Ridge. It began on 8 April, was resumed with a diminished number of tanks on the 11th, but petered out – as far as the tanks were concerned – in terrible weather, poor ground conditions and recriminations from the Australian infantry, who felt they had been let down by the tanks.

In June the scene shifted north to Flanders where an attack was planned against German positions on the Messines and Wytschaete ridges. Mark IV tanks were used for the first time, seventy-six in all, manned by members of A and B battalions, but their efforts were eclipsed by the explosion of a series of huge underground mines which virtually blew the top off the ridge. Tanks were used successfully in a number of minor actions on the day (7 June 1917) but they struggled over difficult ground so the infantry, well supported by the artillery, got ahead of them and took the day's objectives.

By the late summer of 1917 there were nine tank battalions of what was now officially the Tank Corps in France, the last to arrive being the 8th (H) Battalion in August. Much thought was being given to the further expansion of the corps but this came at a time of severe manpower shortage, due to the massive scale of losses on the Somme in 1916 and now in Flanders. This was compounded to some extent by the poor showing of tanks on the saturated, low-lying land around Ypres. Another staff officer, Major J.F.C. Fuller described it thus: 'From the Tank point of view the Third Battle of Ypres is a complete study of how to move thirty tons of metal through a morass of mud and water.' It could hardly have been described better. However, outside the Tank Corps things were seen differently. The external view was that 'tanks cannot operate on bad going; there will always be bad going on a battlefield; ergo tanks will always be useless on a battlefield.' As a result plans to expand the corps were shelved and there was a distinct risk, after such a positive start, that tanks would be a passing fancy, a flash in the pan.

The Third Battle of Ypres began on 31 July 1917 and it was just as Fuller said. Tanks set off for battle but, as the artillery destroyed the drainage and the rain fell in torrents they simply sank into the mud until they could go no further; there were a few highlights but nothing like enough to justify their survival. Then, on 19 August there came a beautifully planned attack which, according to Basil Liddell Hart, helped to save the day. Nine tanks from G Battalion, all with picked crews, took on a nest of German pillboxes near the pulverised village of St Julien which had been holding up progress. By keeping to the roads and literally battering each strongpoint into submission by gunfire the task was achieved in a day with, according to some, just fifteen wounded against a forecast of between 600 and 1,000 casualties from the planners.

> 69986 Gunner Smith, H.E., B Battalion, Awarded Military Medal
>
> Operations in the Ypres Salient, August 19, 1917. For conspicuous gallantry and devotion to duty. When the other gunners of his crew had been knocked out, although himself wounded, he worked the guns in turn, and afterwards helped in driving the tank. He afterwards returned to his gun and fought on the way home. His conduct was exemplary throughout the day.
>
> Tank Corps Book of Honour

Third Ypres ended officially on 9 October 1917 and tanks took part in a number of actions in that time. Most were on a relatively small scale, with limited objectives, some more successful than others but at least the tanks had won a reprieve. Field Marshal Sir Douglas Haig summed it up thus:

> Although throughout the major part of the Ypres battle and especially in its later stages, the condition of the ground made the use of tanks difficult or impossible, yet whenever circumstances were in any way favourable, and even when they were not, very gallant and valuable work had been accomplished by tank commanders and crews on a great number of occasions.

It does help to have friends in high places.

In November 1917 tracks began to stir once again in the Middle East. A new field commander, Sir Edmund Allenby, replaced Sir Archibald Murray and planned to revive the offensive against

Turkish positions at Gaza. Allenby had some experience of tanks at Arras earlier in the year but that had not been very positive so it remained to be seen how he might use them now. In the event the surviving Mark I tanks, brought back up to eight in number by the arrival of some Mark IVs, proved to be of considerable use to the infantry, despite being given a number of extra tasks, and the Gaza position fell after three days' fighting. That, however, was the end of it as far as tanks in the Middle East were concerned, at least for now. The army was moving too fast for the lumbering old tanks to keep up and, when a request for Whippets was turned down in March 1918, this small pioneering force was disbanded.

It remains to mention one more element in the early part of the Tank Corps story: the arrival in France of 1st Gun Carrier Company, although that title was not bestowed until the end of 1917. When they arrived in June and July they were simply known as sections: four of them, labelled A to D. The gun carriers, although similar mechanically to the Mark I tanks were quite different to look at. Indeed they were not tanks at all but what today we might call self-propelled guns. Even then there were differences: unlike modern self-propelled guns, which are effectively artillery pieces on tracks, the gun carriers, as the name implies, were designed to transport guns which were winched aboard or unloaded as required. To that extent they were probably closer to what the French would call portée, although their fate was complicated.

To begin with the crews for these vehicles were formed by Army Service Corps men as drivers, with gunners from the Royal Garrison Artillery to man the guns: either the six-inch howitzer or the long-barrelled sixty-pounder field gun. However, before they saw action the War Office decided that they should be incorporated into the Tank Corps, at least as far as their organisation and the Army Service Corps crews were concerned; this would not affect the Royal Garrison Artillery. As a result, according to some historians, the gun carriers lost their chance to play a significant part in the war – at least as gun carriers. Granted the business of loading and unloading the guns was laborious and time consuming and their effect, in such small numbers, on the course of the battle was insignificant, but given a fair chance they might have done a lot better. As it was, the Tank Corps regarded them as useful and capacious cargo carriers, every bit as useful on the battlefield but not, perhaps, in quite so spectacular a fashion.

The Battle of Cambrai, which began before dawn on 20 November 1917, is regarded by the Royal Tank Regiment as its keynote battle, so much so that 20 November, Cambrai Day, has been celebrated annually ever since. It was not the first tank battle – that, as we have seen, took place more than a year earlier – nor was it the biggest in the First World War (that was yet to come), but it marked a coming of age and an acceptance by the rest of the British Army that the tank was a weapon with potential that was here to stay. So much has been written about Cambrai that there is no need to repeat it here except to say that the demands of this big, set-piece battle saw tank crews adapting to special roles such as dragging away masses of barbed wire to create routes for the cavalry, manning special wireless tanks which set themselves up as reporting stations on the battlefield or towing sledges, loaded with supplies, to areas where other tanks could replenish from them.

Not everyone was a veteran, though – here is the account of a young man with no combat experience at all who joined his battalion just four days before the battle.

On 5 November 1917, just 3 days after my 19th birthday, I landed at Boulogne with a party of about 40 from Wareham. We stayed some days at Le Treport which was the base for Tank Corps personnel. About a dozen of us were posted to H Battalion who were at that time at Wailly near Arras. On 16 November we moved to Dessart Wood near Havrincourt Wood where we set to greasing the many points outside and inside the tank, making sure that the magazines for the Lewis guns were filled and the panniers ready for stacking away in the tank. I was trained as a driver but I had to serve a Lewis gun now.

Private George Brown, H Battalion Tank Corps in H50 *Hurricane*

However, it is again worth emphasising that not every Tank Corps man was a member of a tank crew; the following citation for the

Military Medal applied to two men, gunners Blurton and Wright of 9th (I) Battalion on the 20th: 'For conspicuous gallantry and devotion to duty. At the action near La Vacquerie on November 20 1917, these men acted as orderlies to the company commander. They were continuously taking messages to tanks which were under heavy fire, and were in all cases successful.' Which is to say that they were moving about, on foot, all over the battlefield with shells and bullets flying through the air, going up to tanks – which themselves were the target of every enemy gun in the vicinity – stopping the tank and delivering a message. Not once but all day long.

All nine battalions then in France took part, along with the gun carriers, and history was made when Brigadier General Hugh Elles selected tank H1, *Hilda*, as his mount to lead his new corps into action, flying the brown, red and green flag recently adopted. Those colours, which Fuller decided represented mud, blood and the green fields beyond, remain the distinguishing colour of the Royal Tank Regiment although each battalion had a distinguishing colour of its own, and still does.

Meanwhile new battalions were still being raised at Bovington and their histories are remarkably similar. For example the next four, 10th, 11th, 12th and 13th battalions, were all formed between July and August 1917. All four started out with a nucleus of men from the 'Depot' (i.e. Bovington) but what happened next seems to reflect the prevailing conditions in France. Both 10th and 11th battalions received a draft of some 300 men from the Royal Field Artillery and a similar number of yeomanry but within weeks the latter had been withdrawn and sent to France as infantry. In the case of 10th Battalion these men came from the Westminster Dragoons and Northamptonshire Yeomanry while the 11th received lots of unruly colonials from 2nd King Edward's Horse. In the case of 12th Battalion most of their men came from the Machine Gun Corps Cavalry Depot at Uckfield in Sussex but there is no record of them being posted away. The 13th Battalion is less specific: it says that some men were posted to France as infantry but does not explain where they came from in the first place. These four battalions all moved across to France between December 1917 and January 1918.

In fact the baptism of fire for most of these battalions was not always connected with tanks. The dramatic German offensive of March and April 1918 required every man who could handle a gun and so, apart from drivers who were deemed too valuable, tank crews from both new and existing battalions went into the line as Lewis gun teams with no armour protection at all. Long weeks of fighting, retreating and sometimes dying in desperate last stands took a heavy toll. Tanks were used on occasions: notably at Villers-Bretonneux on 24 April 1918 when the first tank-versus-tank action took place, and a company of Whippets from 3rd Battalion effectively wiped out two German battalions in the open near the village of Cachy.

Whippets were one of four new types of armoured vehicle introduced into the Tank Corps in the summer of 1918. The others were the Mark V heavy tank, the lengthened Mark V* and a small number of Austin armoured cars issued to the 17th (Armoured Car) Battalion. Manufacturing capacity had also been expanded. Factories in Glasgow, Newcastle upon Tyne, Leeds and Gainsborough joined in the production programme, while capacity was also increased at Birmingham. As the Allies recovered from the German onslaught they started to strike back and, following some quite focussed battles in July the corps came together for a massive onslaught against the Germans at Amiens which began on 8 August 1918. A total of 580 tanks, including reserves, were available and by employing the Cambrai formula on an even larger scale the success was proportionately greater – '. . . the Black Day of the German Army,' General Erich Ludendorff called it.

From 8 August until 11 November, inaccurately referred to as the 'Hundred Days', the Germans were in almost constant retreat with the Allies, including their tanks, on their heels. The end was in sight, but it would not all be plain sailing. This account, by Captain D.E. Hickey, concerns his section of three tanks from 8th (H) Battalion and a failed night attack with 10th Australian Infantry Brigade on the night of 10 August 1918:

> After about half-an-hour there was a short lull, except for desultory firing. The tanks had halted. The Colonel was on the road taking stock of the situation, and I was hurriedly

approaching the rear tank when the tank commander of H25 hastened to me with a terrific wound in his right fore-arm . . . He reported that the enemy were using anti-tank rifles and armour piercing bullets . . . I immediately returned to the colonel to tell him that I have lost an officer . . .

The tanks started to move again. Immediately there was a hurricane of machine-gun fire, and we again took cover. The night was pitch-black, except for occasional flares . . .

I discovered that the officer in charge of tank H24 had been killed during the first few minutes of the engagement while walking outside his tank to keep in touch with the infantry. The tank was perforated on all sides by armour-piercing bullets, and all the crew, except two, were wounded. The tank was now in charge of the second driver, a gunner, who had manoeuvred it for position to engage enemy machine-guns from what appeared to be a strong point. It was this manoeuvre which the infantry mistook and led them to report that the tank was returning.

By the time the next four battalions were formed things had changed, no doubt as a result of Cambrai. The 14th Battalion records that most of its men came from the infantry in France but also explains that one company was detached for service in Ireland where things were hotting up; what they actually did there is not clear. They were ready to go to France in the spring of 1918, which was the time of the great German offensive. Having trained hard on their tanks they did not relish going into the line as machine-gun troops – as many of the Tank Corps personnel already in France had done – so they continued tank training in locations around the Bovington area, at Bloxworth and Stoborough, ultimately going across to France in June 1918 when things had quietened down. The 15th Battalion, which was formed at Bovington in January 1918, must have had a unique character since the majority of its men came from Scottish infantry regiments, bolstered by some Royal Engineers. It went over to France in July 1918 but later complained that many experienced tank men were removed from the battalion and shipped back to Britain to form the nucleus of new battalions still being raised. Many of the men drafted in to take their place were miners, another trend brought about by the desperate man-power situation.

Two other battalions, the 16th and 18th, trained at Bovington and went to France in time to see some action in the final weeks of the war but the middle one, the 17th Battalion, had a most unusual fate. Ordained originally to be a light battalion in Whippet tanks, it was actually constituted at Bovington, on 16 April 1918, as an armoured car battalion equipped with redundant Austin armoured cars from a Russian order. These were brought from Bulford in Wiltshire to Bovington on the 19th and organised into two companies, each of four sections of two cars each, making eight cars per company and sixteen for the whole battalion. As a result the 17th battalion was much smaller, in terms of manpower, than a conventional tank battalion but it led a lively and interesting existence. The other Austins at Bulford went to equip Duncars in Iraq, as mentioned in the previous chapter.

An Austin armoured car of 17th (Armoured Car) Battalion, Tank Corps with its very relaxed crew. Note the distinctive camouflage scheme.

The 3rd Battalion band, probably photographed at Bovington towards the end of the war or just after.

It is probably worth remarking, at this point, that a number of tank battalions styled 'light' were in fact equipped with typical heavy tanks to begin with, pending delivery of new models. In practice there were only ever two battalions, the 3rd and the 6th, that were actually equipped with the lighter Whippet tanks during the war although the 9th Battalion had a few before it was converted to Mark Vs. It is also worth noting that, despite the fact that a Whippet tank required roughly half the crew of a heavy tank, the manpower of these battalions remained the same. The reason was that conditions in the Whippets were so dreadful that it was found easier to retain two crews per tank, working turn and turn about, because, after a day's action a crew would be too debilitated to carry on. For example, 6th (F) Battalion records that it had A and B crews for each of its Whippets: the A crew consisted of an officer and two men, the B crew an NCO and two men and they operated the same tank on alternate days.

The final eight battalions, the 19th to 26th, never left Bovington. Such history as they have is so similar that one can generalise, but it is worth noting how the personnel who came to them reflect the changing situation. On the one hand plans for 1919 required many more tank battalions but manpower resources were diminishing to the extent that the authorities were prepared to call up men from previously reserved occupations. On average these men formed 70 per cent of a new battalion. They were, in the main, agricultural workers, railway workers and miners – Welsh miners according to 23rd Battalion – most of whom had been recruited into the cavalry and Royal Field Artillery over the previous two months but had never been abroad on service. The 19th battalion described many of their men as 'elderly' although that might be a relative term. The remain-ing 30 per cent, who were often late arrivals, were mostly experienced NCOs and some drivers from the Tank Corps battalions in France. In fact, no sooner had the training begun than the Armistice came into effect and the long process of demobilisation began. Agricultural workers, particularly ploughmen, were needed back on the land while most of the railwaymen were sent to the Railway Operating Division Training Centre at Bordon in Hampshire to be evaluated.

In 1916 the War Office decided to create a new series of officer cadet training battalions in an effort to overcome the critical shortage of officers and create opportunities for men of wider backgrounds than the traditional British Army officer. In 1918 a dedicated Tank Corps officer cadet battalion – the 24th – was established at Hazeley Down near Winchester. Cadets, who could be identified by a broad white band around their service caps, could be anything from young men, fresh from school, to older men such as aspiring NCOs from regiments in France who hoped to gain a commission and a place in the Tank Corps.

Another group not directly connected with the Tank Corps who deserve to be mentioned are the young women of Queen Mary's Army Auxiliary Corps, which maintained a depot in Swanage and provided girls to undertake all kinds of domestic duties at Bovington and other Tank Corps camps in the area. That they were regarded as something more than mere skivvies is indicated by the

Hotchkiss machine-gun instruction for cadets of the 24th Battalion at Hazeley Down Camp, Winchester towards the end of the war.

fact that they can be seen in many photographs wearing the tank crew arm badge: a somewhat improper but very friendly gesture. Swanage also provided a home for the Tank Corps Training and Reinforcement Centre, commanded by Lieutenant Colonel W.

Pepys, which processed new recruits before they were sent to their battalions.

Meanwhile, in the immediate aftermath of war parents began to search for loved ones who, as far as they were aware, were only recorded as missing and pathetic notices such as this started to appear in the corps journal: 'Sec-Lieut F G Sinkinson, No. 2 Tank Battalion, wounded and captured March 23rd 1918; any information

Girls of Queen Mary's Auxiliary Army Corps showing off their Tank Corps arm badges.

will be gratefully received by his parents, Monksfield, Lytham, Lancs.'

Wars, of course, never end tidily: they give rise to other simmering conflicts which demand attention, and while the Armistice held the Tank Corps had many other problems to deal with, in various parts of the world. For example five tank battalions formed part of the Army of Occupation in Germany while the remaining battalions in France were cut down to a basic core – what is called cadre strength – and shipped home. Most of those battalions formed at Bovington that never went abroad simply disappeared.

Yet another unusual tank force came into being at the end of the war. This was a special Royal Engineers detachment based at Christchurch near Bournemouth. It was the brainchild of Major Giffard le Quesne Martel, the Sapper officer who had served with the

Tank Corps during the war. The original plan was to raise three Royal Engineer tank battalions but this was reduced to a company when hostilities ended and it became responsible for experimental modifications to tanks including bridge-laying and mine-sweeping. It was in a very real sense the forerunner of the famous Funnies of the Second World War.

Three British Tank Corps detachments were sent to Russia in 1919 in an effort to bolster the anti-Bolshevik forces but it was a forlorn hope. All of these men were volunteers. The largest by far was the South Russian Tank Detachment. It saw some action but the morale of the troops they were supposed to be training crumbled fast and desertion was endemic. They returned to Britain in June 1920 but left all of their tanks behind. The North West Russian Tank Detachment was based largely in Estonia; their story is similar,

A Mark V* male tank in Dublin with what appears to be an infantry crew. By 1920 the rapidly demobilising army was stretched to find trained tank men to meet emergency situations.

albeit on a smaller scale, and they came back, tankless, in November 1919. The North Russian Tank Detachment, based at Archangel, was even smaller and only there to protect the port facilities. They gave their tanks to the so-called White Russians and sailed home in October 1919.

In due course the forces in Germany were reduced as men went back to their peacetime lives until all that remained was a composite battalion, nominally 12th Battalion based at Solingen, plus what was known as the Rhine Army Tank Company at Cologne. This was relieved by a company from 5th Battalion in April 1920 which briefly became involved in confrontations with the Germans before things quietened down. By this time of course the German government had surrendered although domestic conflicts continued. It was replaced by B Company, 3rd Battalion in November 1923 but at that time there were other changes, revealed in the next chapter.

Meanwhile trouble had flared in Ireland so 17th (Armoured Car) Battalion, which was also in Germany, was despatched to Dublin via Britain in January 1919. Here it expanded and took over some tanks that were already there, based in Dublin and Limerick, but in March

These men, posing with two Rolls-Royce armoured cars belong to a cyclists battalion of the Essex Regiment, probably on home defence duties. It is not easy to date this picture although it does prove that armoured vehicles were issued to many units that were neither Machine Gun Corps nor Tank Corps.

Yellow Wizard, a Rolls-Royce from No. 2 Armoured Car Company in Iraq in 1922. It still sports the LAMB (Light Armoured Motor Battery) symbol of its previous owners in a diamond on the side of the bonnet.

1920 the battalion was reconstituted as 5th Armoured Car Company in keeping with events in Britain.

The situation in Britain in the immediate aftermath of the war is complicated. The Tank Corps was in effect dissolving itself and recreating itself at the same time in order to ensure continuity and meet new demands. A dozen tank battalions sent home from France were reduced to cadre strength, that is to say a small nucleus of experienced regulars. From these, five new battalions were created along with a dozen armoured car companies, most of which went out to the Middle East or India.

The old 1st Battalion, now renamed 1st Depot Battalion, began life at Wareham in July 1919, moving to Bovington in January 1921. The other four, 2nd through to 5th, were also reconstituted around this time. The 2nd Battalion absorbed the personnel from the 20th Battalion while the 4th Battalion took over the 19th Battalion, both of which disappeared, while 3rd Battalion, which reformed but only at cadre strength in November 1919, was sent to Ireland. Meanwhile at Bovington 5th Battalion reformed in September 1919 and, as we have seen, sent a company to Germany the following year. In due course the tank battalions dispersed to stations around southern Britain: the 2nd to Farnborough, the 3rd to Lydd in Kent and the 5th to Tidworth on Salisbury Plain. These would remain their home stations throughout the inter-war years.

A national coal strike, called in March 1921 and which ran on for about six weeks, saw over 600 men called back to the colours. The Tank Corps raised a number of temporary units that were sent to locations all around the country. Armoured cars were preferred, being seen as less heavy-handed than tanks, but tanks were sent to some locations where serious trouble was anticipated. In the event nothing happened that required their services.

Armoured car companies were, with one exception, something quite new to the Tank Corps. Most were formed in Britain and the majority ended up in various parts of the Middle East, including Egypt, Palestine and Mesopotamia (Iraq). In the main they took over the cars, and sometimes personnel, from units already operating out there. Demobilisation had played havoc with the previous units, particularly in Iraq, and quite often men were drafted in from other branches of the army just to make up numbers. About 2,000 men, in Britain and elsewhere, were transferred to the Tank Corps in 1922 when the original Machine Gun Corps, foster parent of the Tank Corps, was disbanded.

The situation in India was similar. Until the Tank Corps took over in February 1920 the existing armoured car units only kept going by drafting personnel from the infantry but the situation on the North-West Frontier and in particular fresh trouble with Afghanistan, in what was known officially as the Third Afghan War, in 1919 placed even greater demand on manpower. From 1920 Tank Corps personnel from Britain and Iraq manned eight armoured car companies, mostly using vehicles already in the country.

The Tank Corps had no direct association with the Territorial

The crew of this smart, Peerless armoured car proudly show off some of its features to an enthusiastic audience. The men are from the 23rd Armoured Car Company, Royal Tank Corps, popularly known as the 'Sharpshooters'.

Army during the war and indeed, in the case of the infantry, the difference between the Territorials and the regulars was largely buried during the war. In order to sort things out the Territorial Army was effectively closed down in 1919 and reconstituted in 1920. The cavalry element in the Territorial Army was the yeomanry and eight of these regiments were converted to Tank Corps armoured car companies between 1920 and 1922. These were:

19th ACC Lothians and Border Horse
20th ACC Fife and Forfar Yeomanry
21st ACC Gloucestershire Yeomanry
22nd ACC 2nd County of London Yeomanry (Westminster
    Dragoons)

23rd ACC 3rd County of London Yeomanry (Sharpshooters)
24th ACC Derbyshire Yeomanry
25th ACC Northamptonshire Yeomanry
26th ACC East Riding of Yorkshire Yeomanry

These men retained their cap badges but in all other respects wore the same uniform and distinguishing details of the Tank Corps. The following account, concerning 24th Armoured Car Company, the Derbyshire Yeomanry, gives a flavour of these early days:

> Let us take, as an example of what we were at that time, a typical summer camp in any of the years between the wars. Twelve officers and about 145 men would assemble, usually at some seaside resort, and for the next fourteen days would spend a very pleasant holiday under canvas. About a dozen 1920 model Rolls-Royce armoured cars would have been obtained from the pool kept for that purpose, and under regular drivers – for we could not raise twelve good enough drivers of our own – would have arrived in camp, if they were lucky! The first week in camp was confined to Troop training, and during the final week we reached the dizzy heights of Squadron training. Practically all work ceased at 4 p.m. and the remainder of the day was given over to sports, concerts, sing-songs, etc. At the end of the fortnight all would return, except those in hospital, to their homes, sunburnt, happy and a little, but not much, wiser.
>
> During the winter months a few individual drills would take place either at 91 Siddals Road, Derby or in Ashbourne, when the main topic of conversation would be the next year's camp.
>
> Ian Walker, 1st Derbyshire Yeomanry

Resources to Help Find Your First World War Tank Ancestor

The resources listed below will refer to those connected with tanks during the First World War and will cover the Machine Gun Corps Heavy Branch/Section and the Tank Corps, but, as explained earlier, just because your ancestor was 'in tanks' did not necessarily mean he served with the Tank Corps – even if he did then he more than likely served with a different regiment prior to this. Checking his cap badge and uniform will help identify which regiment he served with, but this may only be possible if photographs of him in uniform have survived. Another point to remember is that even if he did serve with the Tank Corps he may not have been part of the active tank company but part of the support network surrounding it.

Initially then a search should be made at The National Archives for any records that may be relevant to your ancestor's service. These include:

> Personal visit:
> Campaign Medal Roll (WO329)
> Officer Service Records (WO339 and WO374)

> Online:
> www.documentsonline.nationalarchives.gov.uk for Medal Index
>   Cards (WO 372) for campaign and gallantry awards
> Index to Officer Service Records (WO 338)

In conjunction with www.ancestry.co.uk the following non-commissioned and other ranks documents can also be searched online:

> Surviving Service Records (WO363)
> Pension Records (WO364)
> Campaign Medal Cards

Once these sources have been exhausted the following documents and books will help you fill out your ancestor's story or even find further references to him.

Documents

War Diaries

War Diaries are the daily operational reports of all regiments and are the closest and most contemporary accounts of where and what a regiment was doing. The National Archives and the Tank Museum hold the Tank Corps/Heavy Branch, Machine Gun Corps War Diaries. Initially battalions were known by letters (e.g. A

Battalion) but from January 1918 this changed to numbers (e.g. 1st Battalion). For a while both were used simultaneously (e.g. A/1st Battalion). All Tank Corps War Diaries at the Tank Museum (A/1st Battalion to the 26th Battalion, including Tank Carrier Companies) have been transcribed. Unfortunately during the First World War it was generally only officers who were mentioned in the War Diaries.

Personal Papers

The Tank Museum has many personal accounts typed and recorded, many of which have been transcribed and are in a searchable database in the Archive Reading Room. There is also a collection of personal papers ranging from pay books to training documents and below is a small selection.

> A collection of documents relating to William Scott of C/3rd Battalion, Tank Corps includes his soldier's pay book but also a couple of Old Comrades Association members lists dated 1921 and 1925. (TM E1969.98.1.3)

> Various certificates of congratulations from Major General Sir Hugh Elles, commanding the Tank Corps in France. One to Private John A. Witty talks about his 'pluck and good driving in action against the enemy . . .' (TM E1988.14.2)

> A notebook/diary, complete with bullet hole, belonging to C.A. Ironmonger, D/4th Battalion, Tank Corps, which includes a variety of crew names. Corporal Ironmonger's life was saved by the book, when he was shot leaving his tank. (TM E2003.1190)

> A notebook belonging to Captain A. Graham Woods, Adjutant, D Company, Heavy Section, Machine Gun Corps, which lists crews and tank numbers and is dated 1916. (TM E1963.38.1)

> A National Registration Act, 1915 card for George Richard Farrin (TM E1976.102.1) and a permit book for Wilfred Head, used for permission to carry a camera (TM E1995.17.14.1), are typical of the variety of documents available.

Official Documents

As well as the War Diaries, the Tank Museum holds other official documents. An example is a Company Roll Book for the 18th Company, F Battalion, for the summer of 1917 and 20–27 November 1917 (Battle of Cambrai). The booklet is handwritten by Major P. Hamond and includes such details as name, rank and number, occupation and address, the nature of a casualty, medals awarded and action or reserve. Crews are listed by number of tank, e.g. No. 9 Section, Crew F41 (TM E2005.51). Another example is Nominal Rolls 1914–1918, which is the Machine Gun Corps/Tank Corps nominal roll of officers (TM E2008.2207.1–9).

Battle History Sheets

Although battle sheets do not usually include lists of crews, they are a fascinating insight into tanks in battle on a particular day. They give tank number, commander, weather and ground conditions and include casualties. As with all resources, a successful search is dependent on which documents have survived, so some battalions are better served than others. For example, the Tank Museum has a good selection of battle sheets for the 8th Battalion for 1918 (TM E2007.7*) and other examples can be found at the Imperial War Museum.

Books

Below is a selection of books that might be useful to you in your search although it is by no means comprehensive. Many will have been out of print for many years and may not be easily found, although some have been reprinted. Your local library is a good start for trying to get hold of a copy through the British Library and many go for huge amounts of money on eBay. The Tank Museum Archive and Reference Library has copies of all the mentioned books and I am sure that other large repositories such as the Liddell Hart Centre in London will also have copies.

Maurice, Major R.F.G., *The Tank Corps Book of Honour* **(Spottiswoode, Ballantyne & Co Ltd, 1919)**
The Tank Corps Book of Honour was produced after the war to

record the deeds and the awards of Tank Corps members. It is arranged by date of battle as it says in the Preface 'to trace the growth of the new arm from its first appearance in the field to that final victory'. It records in detail the awards of the four Victoria Cross holders:

Captain Clement Robertson, 1st Battalion
Lieutenant (Acting Captain) Richard W.L. Wain, 1st Battalion
Lieutenant Cecil H. Sewell, 3rd Battalion
Captain (Acting Lieutenant Colonel) Richard A. West, 6th Battalion

It includes all awards made, both immediate (action in the field) and other honours, and also includes a Roll of Honour for those who were killed. It does not include individual Mentions in Despatches or any list for those who were wounded.

The War History of the Sixth Tank Battalion, (Privately printed, 1919)

This book gives a comprehensive account of the 6th or 'F' Battalion's actions in the First World War. It is especially useful for the family historian, as it lists in Appendix III all the officers and men who served with the battalion in France. This is unusual, as in most cases it is only the officers who are listed and the men only if they were killed or won an award. It also gives their service numbers. Appendix I lists honours and awards and Appendix II lists dates of actions of the battalion.

The other unusual feature of the history is that within the book, the wounded, injured and missing are also listed along with those killed in that particular action. The fact that it was written immediately after the war also adds to its authenticity.

Both of the following books cover specific battles during the First World War, but they are both well researched from original sources and can be considered as accurate accounts as possible given the resources available.

Pidgeon, Trevor, *The Tanks at Flers: An Account of the First Use of Tanks in War at the Battle of Flers-Courcelette, The Somme, 15th September 1916*, 2 volumes, (Fairmile Books, 1995, ISBN 0 9525175 0 7)

This two-volume set of books is a very thorough account of the first tank battle and the second volume is devoted entirely to detailed maps of the area. Its main value to family historians, however, is in the first volume, which includes maps, first-hand accounts and photographs. Appendix 1 lists the officers and men who served at that time with C and D battalions, Heavy Section, Machine Gun Corps. The additional value of these lists is that they are split into sections and even by tank numbers and names, so it could be possible to find which tank your ancestor was in during the battle. The number on a tank started with the letter of the battalion and consequently the naming of tanks generally also started with the letter of the battalion e.g. C1 721 'Champagne' for a tank of C Battalion and D9 546 'Dolly' for D Battalion.

Gibot, Jean-Luc and Gorczynski, Philippe, *Following the Tanks: Cambrai 20 November–7 December 1917,* **translated into English by Wendy McAdam, (Privately published, 1999, ISBN 2 9511696 1 2)**
This book looks at the Battle of Cambrai, which saw the first use of tanks in large numbers (over 300) and was so successful that even today the Royal Tank Regiment honours the battle every year in November and pilgrimages are made to the battlefield.

The book includes the Order of Battle for tanks on the 20 November, as well as for infantry divisions and cavalry corps. The Order of Battle for tanks covers A to I battalions, splits them into companies and sections and gives individual tank numbers and names. It also includes the tank commander's name, but not the rest of the men. Appendix V lists all honours and awards of officers and men and there is a Roll of Honour in Appendix VI, which lists those killed, by battalion, including where they are buried or their memorial. This book also includes photographs, maps and personal accounts.

Soldiers Died in the Great War 1914–19. Part 75: Machine Gun Corps and Tank Corps, **(J.B. Hayward & Son, 1989, ISBN 1 871505 75 5)**
This book lists, for each entry, the place of enlistment, their service number, the date they were killed and their former regiment.

A Short History of the 2nd Battalion Tank Corps in the Great War **(1925)**
Lists honours and awards for both officers and men.

Verrinder, Ian, *Tank Action in the Great War: B Battalion's Experiences 1917* **(Pen & Sword, 2009, ISBN 978 1 84884 080 5)**
Although this book largely only covers 1917, the Order of Battle, crew details, awards and Roll of Honour are an excellent source of information. Crew are listed under the name of their tank and notes added as to their fate, e.g. wounded, killed or survived.

Narrative History of 'G' and 7th Battalion **Gale & Polden, Aldershot, 1919)**
Lists honours and awards for officers and non-commissioned officers.

Maurice, Major F., MC, *The History of the 13th Tank Battalion,* **(Andrew Melrose Ltd, 1920)**
Lists honours and awards; the Roll of Honour includes wounded and missing, as well as killed. A nominal roll of officers gives a brief synopsis of their service.

History of the Fourteenth Battalion Tank Corps
Includes lists of section commanders on the battalion's arrival in France 18 June 1918, and also for 8 August, 27 August and 2 September 1918. Casualties, killed, wounded and missing are also listed, but only officers are named. There is also a list of officers for 20 November 1918.

Operations of the 17th (Armoured Car) Tank Battalion During the Battle of 1918: Compiled from Original Notes and Accounts May 1919 **(Gale & Polden Ltd, 1920)**
Lists officers who served with the battalion including some service notes. Also includes a list of honours. Casualties include killed, wounded, missing and prisoners of war.

Checking cap badges and uniforms will give you a clue to the regiment that your ancestor served with. Two books which are particularly useful if you are struggling with badges and uniforms are:

Windrow, Martin, *Tank and AFV Crew Uniforms since 1916,* **(Patrick Stephens, 1979, ISBN 0 85059 362 X)**
This book covers the period from 1916 to the 1970s for all countries, although the later years are less comprehensive.

Forty, George, *The Royal Tank Regiment: A Pictorial History 1916–2001,* **(Halsgrove, 2001, ISBN 1 84114124 0)**
This book also covers an extensive period, but is good on explaining Royal Tank Regiment traditions and the changes in organisation and insignia.

Other useful books:
Woolnough, F.G., LCP, *A Brief History of The Royal Tank Corps,* **(Gale & Polden Ltd, 1925)**
This is quite a small book, which is a general history of the actions of the Tank Corps in the First World War. Citations for the four VCs are included and the total number of awards made to the corps, but no other names are mentioned.

A Short History of the Royal Tank Corps, **(Gale & Polden Ltd, various editions from 1930 to 1945)**
This history covers the actions of the Tank Corps from the First World War to eventually 1938, as information is added with every new edition. For instance 'Important dates in the History of the Royal Tank Corps' covers 1914 to 1936 in the sixth edition and 'The Formation of the Royal Tank Corps', which in effect is a chart showing where each battalion was at a given date, extends to 1938 in the 1945 edition. Lists of commanders are also included, as well as a summary of awards.

Liddell Hart, Captain B.H., *The Tanks: The History of the Royal Tank Regiment,* **2 volumes, (Cassell & Co Ltd, 1959). Volume One: 1914–1939; Volume Two: 1939–1945.**
The regimental history of the Royal Tank Regiment from the

development of the tank through to the operations and actions of the Tank Corps/Regiment.

Williams-Ellis, Major Clough, MC and Ellis, A. Williams, *The Tank Corps*, (Country Life, 1919)

Wilson, C. Murray, *Fighting Tanks* (Seeley, Service & Co. Ltd, 1929)

Charteris, Captain Evan, *H.Q. Tanks* (Privately Printed, 1920)

Browne, Captain, *The Tank In Action, William Blackwood & Sons, 1920*

Forty, George and Forty, Anne, *Bovington Tanks*, (Wincanton Press, 1988, ISBN 0 902129 97X)
This book looks at Bovington Camp, including Lulworth Camp and the surrounding area, from its early days through to 1988. It includes many photographs and a map of 'Tintown', 1930. It is useful because it covers the 'at home' part of a soldiers life, which was largely dominated by training.

Other Resources
Other resources which might prove useful are:

CD-ROM 'Soldiers who died in the Great War 1914–1919' (Naval & Military Press, 1998)

Photographs
Thousands of photographs are available at the Imperial War Museum and the Tank Museum, as well as many other repositories. Identifying armoured vehicles is probably easier than identifying unnamed people, so although photographs can be an excellent visual source, without names attached they can be of minimal value. Group photographs are often more interesting than individual photographs, although as we have already seen photographs are useful for spotting badges and thus identifying regiments.

Journals

Tank Corps Journal (1919 to date)

The *Tank Journal* has been published by the Royal Tank Regiment and its predecessors since 1919, changing its name with the changing corps name, so in 1919 it was the *Tank Corps Journal*, followed by the *Royal Tank Corps Journal* from 1923 to 1939 and finally as *The Tank*. It was originally published monthly then quarterly but this has recently been reduced to three times a year.

It contains a wealth of information from operations, promotions, sporting events through to obituaries, which would be difficult to obtain elsewhere and although it is not indexed to any degree, plans are being made to digitise the contents.

The Western Front Association (www.westernfrontassociation. com)

The Association was founded to encourage interest in the First World War and produces a journal and a bulletin. There are numerous branches across the country, which offer talks on various subjects related to the war.

Chapter 3

THE ROYAL TANK CORPS
1923–1939

Army Order No. 369 of 1923 read:-

GEORGE R. I.

Whereas we have noted with great satisfaction the splendid work that has been performed by Our Tank Corps during the Great War.

Our Will and Pleasure is that the Corps shall enjoy the distinction of 'ROYAL' and shall henceforth be known as Our 'Royal Tank Corps'.

Given at Our Court at St. James's this 18th Day of October, 1923, in the 14th year of Our Reign.

By His Majesty's Command. DERBY

The Tank Corps was gone – the title had no further relevance. In future it would be known as the Royal Tank Corps. It was an auspicious moment, its status as a regular corps had been confirmed just a month previously and the royal accolade clearly bolstered this. The event was marked by the adoption of a new badge and on these early examples the tank, within the laurel wreath, points to the right, as it did on the old Tank Corps badge. This is quite important from a research point of view. If the soldier in the photograph is wearing the old service dress cap with the Tank Corps badge then the picture can be dated at least no later than November 1923. After that he will be sporting the Royal Tank Corps badge, which should show up, being in white metal rather than bronze.

This group, simply captioned 'The Boys, 1924', is interesting because in theory, by this time they should all have been wearing berets. The badge is also difficult to distinguish but it could be the rare original Royal Tank Corps badge with the tank facing right.

The King, of course, had been colonel-in-chief of the corps since 17 October 1918 while Major General Sir John Capper became colonel commandant on 12 September 1923. A month later Brigadier General Sir Hugh Elles, who had commanded the corps in France since 1917 and the Tank Corps Centre at Bovington afterwards, relinquished his connection with tanks on being given command of an infantry brigade. These high-level moves were of little relevance to the ordinary serving soldier except from the historical perspective when a signature on a document can help to confirm a date or location.

Then, in March 1924 the corps took the revolutionary step of introducing new headgear in the form of a beret – the first time this was worn in the British Army – and it was in black material because, it was said, this would effectively hide oil and grease stains. Unfortunately on account of the way that the beret was worn, pulled down over the right ear, the tank on the cap badge appeared to be retreating. This was considered unacceptable and the badge was redesigned with the tank facing to the left (as you look at it) so if you can pick out this detail on a photograph it provides another clue to an accurate date.

On 31 May 1925 the Royal Tank Corps Workshops Training Battalion at Bovington was disbanded and the tasks of repair and maintenance of all vehicles passed over to the Royal Army Ordnance Corps. The RAOC also became responsible for issuing vehicles so it is possible to find photographs of men with a strange cap badge on a service dress cap working with tanks from that date onwards.

A month later, on 18 June 1925 to be precise, the title 1st (Depot) Battalion was dropped in favour of Royal Tank Corps Depot. At about the same time 4th Battalion, Royal Tank Corps, which had hitherto been based at Worgret Camp, Wareham moved to Bovington because Worgret was closed down. In March 1926 4th Battalion left Bovington for Catterick in Yorkshire.

It takes nearly two years to make a man into a really tip-top tank driver. But while mentioning that, it is necessary also to mention that there are no specialists in the Royal Tank Corps.

Three men from 4th Battalion, Royal Tank Corps, which was based at Catterick in Yorkshire from about 1931, with their medium tanks in the background sporting the regiment's distinctive Chinese Eye on the turret.

> Every man has to be able to do everything, from manning the guns or driving the tank, to setting a course across country and getting there.
>
> *Yorkshire Evening Post,* following a visit to 4th Battalion at Catterick in 1928

In 1926 B Company, 3rd Battalion, Royal Tank Corps pulled out of Cologne along with the remainder of the British Army, although a section of armoured cars remained at Wiesbaden; then in May a general strike was called in Britain. Tanks and armoured cars had been used on internal security duties during earlier instances of industrial unrest but the perceived scale of this threat may be judged by the fact that elements from 2nd and 3rd battalions, along with men from the Royal Tank Corps schools at Bovington were moved to

Chelsea Barracks in London, while 12th Armoured Car Company, which had been stationed in Belfast, was shipped across to Warrington on Merseyside. The strike only lasted for the first twelve days of the month and the troops returned to their stations, all except 12th ACC, which remained in Warrington until September, after which it came to Bovington.

Armies have indulged in field days, manoeuvres and mock battles almost since the dawn of time but with the appearance of the tank, its mobility and tactical potential needed to be explored. Tanks had participated in a number of exercises since the war, but in 1927 the War Office announced that a major exercise, to be called the Experimental Mechanised Force, would be tried out in southern England, largely on Salisbury Plain. The idea, as the title implies, was to test the viability of a combined force of all arms in vehicles –

These men, filling the belts for their Vickers machine guns, have white patches on their berets, matching the white fabric wrapped around their tank turrets. This might indicate that they represented 'enemy' troops in an exercise.

armoured, artillery, infantry and engineers – against a conventional force of marching soldiers, mounted cavalry and horse-drawn artillery.

It was followed a year later by the Experimental Armoured Force and in both cases the results were, predictably, the same. Given freedom of movement the mechanised army always defeated the conventional one. The exercises attracted a lot of public interest. They were reported like sporting events in the newspapers and were filmed extensively for the cinema newsreels. From the Royal Tank Corps' point of view they involved the 5th Battalion and a selection of armoured cars and light carriers from the 3rd Battalion, although it is worth pointing out that, in 1928 at least, the medium tanks of 3rd Battalion took part in the Essex manoeuvres while 2nd Battalion did similar work in Sussex, It all helped to keep the tanks in the public eye but it is worth noting that one significant element of the army was not involved – the cavalry. And that said a lot about the ruling attitude to armoured warfare at an important level in the military hierarchy.

A tank testing section had been established at Farnborough in 1921, originally under the control of the 2nd Battalion. It grew rapidly and by 1928, now known as the Mechanical Warfare Experimental Establishment, it was responsible for testing and evaluating vehicles of all kinds for all three services, the Overseas Development Corporation and even the Royal National Lifeboat Institution. It was never exclusively Royal Tank Corps, although men in black berets often feature in surviving photographs in the driver's seats of all sorts of vehicles. Subsequently MWEE absorbed the establishment at Christchurch that was mentioned earlier, although it now concentrated primarily on military bridging and was, indeed, the birthplace of the famous Bailey bridge.

Much has been written and said about the mechanisation or 'mechanicalisation' of the cavalry as it is sometimes termed. And it is portrayed in highly emotional terms. The fact is that even the most elite of cavalry regiments had been experiencing drastic change ever since the turn of the century. Gaudy uniforms, now only used for ceremonial purposes, had given way to the drab monotony of khaki, flashing blades to carbines and revolvers and, during what was now

The 12th Royal Lancers were in Egypt when the order came to give up their horses and take up motor vehicles instead. Here they are with an Austin Seven, a Rolls-Royce armoured car and a motorcycle.

referred to as the Great War, the spectacle of cavalrymen lining the trenches alongside their infantry comrades – when opportunities for mounted action were so limited, at least on the Western Front – was now becoming a thing of the past.

Then again, although in action the men would ride horses, regimental transport was changing rapidly from horse drawn to motorised, while the young officers who were so happy to parade in smart uniforms on well-groomed horses drove fast cars in their civilian lives. That the cavalry was reluctant to change was evident soon after the war when a proposal to have them take over the Royal Tank Corps and dominate a new Royal Armoured Corps was rejected, but the writing was on the wall.

In 1922 there were major changes when a number of cavalry

regiments were amalgamated, resulting in such 'vulgar fractions' as the 4th/7th Dragoon Guards, 13th/18th Hussars and 16th/5th Lancers, but still they remained mounted. In fact it was 1928 before the first two cavalry regiments exchanged their horses for armoured vehicles – armoured cars in this case. The chosen regiments were the 11th Hussars in Britain and the 12th Lancers then in Egypt, the two most junior cavalry regiments not to be involved in the 1922 amalgamations. In both cases, by all accounts, the changes were accepted in a positive manner by all ranks.

In fact the delivery of armoured cars was painfully slow and even by 1929, when the regiment had moved to Tidworth on Salisbury Plain, they did not have their full complement, nor indeed garages to put them in. Nevertheless they took part in the cavalry brigade manoeuvres that year and earned glowing compliments:

> The turnout of the men was extremely good. This and the general smartness of their parade work reflects the excellent spirit which prevails throughout the Regiment and demonstrates the satisfactory manner in which all ranks are taking to their new organisation and role.
>
> A.E.W. Harman, Inspector of Cavalry, 1929

However, notice that no mention of armoured cars is actually made.

Incidentally, when the 11th Hussars (the 'Cherrypickers') mechanised in 1928 they also adopted a beret as the headdress for their armoured car crews and they selected a light brown with a cherry red band around the bottom. This was regarded as so distinctive that the King agreed that they need not attach a cap badge at all.

Of course at this time the cavalry was still a thing apart, not affiliated in any way to the Royal Tank Corps except inasmuch as Royal Tank Corps personnel helped to train the cavalrymen on their new equipment. For the next few years, as far as the Royal Tank Corps was concerned, there were no major changes in the United Kingdom apart from the re-creation in 1934 of a genuine 1st Battalion, now known as the 1st (Light) Battalion and based at Perham Down on Salisbury Plain. The battalions remained based at their home stations and the only excitement, in the early thirties at

The 12th Lancers came home at the end of 1934 and took over the huge Lanchester armoured cars of the 11th Hussars, one of which is getting the full treatment here.

least, was the annual training, which had more to do with the organisation of battalions, now organised into brigades, and the tactical lessons that could be derived from new equipment and technological advances such as the introduction of voice radio.

By the early thirties, unemployment was high so the recruiting authorities became more fussy. For example, R.W. Munns, who joined up in 1931, had set his heart on the Royal Navy but was rejected on account of his teeth. However, he was accepted by the army and signed on for six years' service and six more years in the reserve. He seems to have had no choice in what regiment he joined; he was totally ignorant of the existence of the Royal Tank Corps but was posted to it anyway and sent down to Dorset. At Bovington he did his basic training and then went down to Lulworth to learn the skills of tank gunnery:

Training consisted of learning how to fire a 3 pdr [three-pounder: 47mm] gun fitted in a Medium Tank, with a machine-gun fitted co-axially. Using the same trigger mechanism one could fire a 3 pdr shell, or by movement of the co-axial lever a Vickers machine-gun . . .

I suppose there was an element of danger in teaching young recruits to fire a 3 pdr shell from a moving tank. Fortunately 357 Squad completed their gunnery training without mishap, but an earlier Squad nearly demolished the Officers Mess. The 3 pdr was fired from a tank on four sides of a square run, each side being about half a mile in length . . .

Postings were made to all the battalions, and I, and three others were posted to the 3rd Battalion at Lydd.

Abroad it was a different matter. In Iraq there were three armoured car companies, the 1st, 2nd and 6th, responsible for security in a vast region. A lot of interesting work was done operating armoured cars in conjunction with aircraft but other tours, or reconnaissances, were made which relied on terrestrial resupply. In the end, however, the combined armoured car and aircraft operations proved so successful that it was decided to hand over responsibility for security in Iraq to the Royal Air Force who still needed a presence on the ground and took over the armoured cars of 1st and 2nd ACC. This took place between May and July 1922 and by May 1923 the men from these companies had returned to Britain and their units disbanded. The men from 6th ACC had already gone to India while their cars were despatched to Egypt.

The situation in Egypt and the Sudan meant that 3rd Armoured Car Company was severely stretched. Its companion 4th Armoured Car Company spent most of its short life in Palestine, with a long excursion to Baghdad but it was disbanded in July 1922 when the RAF took over. In 1926 the 3rd ACC was reinforced by a section of medium tanks from 3rd Battalion in Britain and in 1929 by 5th ACC, which was returning from China. The mechanisation of the 12th Lancers, already referred to, was achieved over the next two years by passing over the Rolls-Royces from 3rd and 5th ACC; on 1 April 1933 it became the new 6th Battalion, Royal Tank Corps.

The caption to this picture simply says 'Jack in Cairo' but it is full of information. Jack is a corporal, the crossed-swords emblem is a proficiency badge, probably indicating in this case that Jack was a physical training instructor. He also displays his tank crew arm badge, the letters RTC in brass on his epaulette and Royal Tank Corps collar dogs, like small versions of the cap badge.

In 1932, as a test of their newly learned skills, the 12th Lancers mounted a major exercise into the Egyptian desert as far as the Siwa Oasis, concerning which a remarkable and lavish book was produced (*From Cairo to Siwa* by T.L. Dun (E & R Schindler, Cairo, 1933)). This fascination with the desert not only attracted similar expeditions to test equipment and navigation skills, many of which included Royal Tank Corps personnel, but also attracted individuals with an adventurous bent who would rather spend their leave exploring these barren regions than come home to relax in Britain.

The Italian attack on Abyssinia seemed to pose a threat to Egypt and reinforcements were hurried out, including the 1st (Light) Tank Battalion, part of 4th (Army) Tank Battalion and 12th Lancers from Britain. Meanwhile the 8th Hussars, until then a mounted regiment, was training to convert in Cairo, assisted by the 11th Hussars. Since no more armoured cars were available the 8th, for the time being, were equipped with unarmoured pick-up trucks. Within a year the scare had died down and the regiments sent out from Britain returned home, though peace remained elusive. In 1936 events in Palestine required the attention of the 11th Hussars and a company of light tanks from 6th Battalion, Royal Tank Corps, among other forces, but this was largely settled by the end of the year.

India was another problem altogether. Trouble was endemic and the Royal Tank Corps armoured car companies – of which there were eight in the country at one time plus a headquarters at Ahmednagar – were much in demand. The companies moved around India from time to time and from the mid-thirties were gradually reclassified as light tank companies – six in all – although some never got light tanks at all. The arrangements for exchanging men from their parent battalions at home to temporary postings with the companies in India is not entirely clear. There appears to be no correlation between the battalion they served with in Britain and the company they were posted to in India, although when returning home men usually went back to their original battalion. On the outbreak of war in 1939 these companies were still in the process of handing over to Indian Army regiments.

Although trouble could flare up anywhere in India the most renowned trouble spot of all was, and always has been, the North-

Regimental badges were not worn on the sola topee (sun helmet) but in this studio shot of Private Hillyard we can see the topee flash, in Royal Tank Corps colours and the letters 3ACC indicating that he was serving with 3rd Armoured Car Company. This picture was taken in India, but similar conditions applied in the Middle East.

West Frontier and in particular the tribal territories that lay between India proper and the Afghan frontier. In order to keep the lid on potential trouble the British Army established a series of fortified camps, mostly at existing settlements, linked by a circular road. Right in the centre, in Waziristan, was Razmak, an entirely artificial settlement with a very high security perimeter, described by one British soldier as the most isolated monastery in the world: no women were permitted there and it was unsafe to leave the camp except as part of a military expedition. It was a huge camp, brigade sized, housing up to 10,000 men, both British and native troops supported by an armoured car company of the Royal Tank Corps.

One armoured car company of sixteen vehicles, usually Crossleys, was always stationed there and the arrangement was that one section was always held at almost instant readiness while another would take a little longer to be ready for action. A third section was located about fifteen miles away along the road at a camp called Razani. The armoured cars were used to escort convoys and any other vulnerable travellers such as the field cashier or VIP visitors, although these were rare. Razmak could hardly be described as typical – indeed it was probably one of the most extreme of all the frontier stations occupied by the Royal Tank Corps – but it was at the heart of where the action was, a place where armoured cars were retained, virtually on a war footing and on active service nearly all the time.

> It had been decided that the Company in Waziristan should serve there for one year only and that at Peshawar for two years, all the others being three year stations. These arrangements, however, proved very elastic in practice and in the early years the service of the two North West Frontier companies was often prolonged beyond the terms laid down. Although the companies frequently changed stations within India, all of them remained in the country for the whole period between the wars. Their personnel altered of course, annually, as officers and men went back to England on the expiration of their overseas service and were replaced by others sent out from home. Thus there was a constant interchange of

personnel between Tank Battalions at home and Armoured Car Companies in India to the mutual benefit of both.

Major E.W. Sheppard, RTC

Among the overseas adventures it remains to mention China. When the Chinese Civil War threatened to affect the European settlement a Shanghai Defence Force was created, to which 5th Armoured Car Company was attached. They arrived in March 1927 and sailed for Egypt in January 1929 where, as already explained, they ultimately became part of 6th Battalion, Royal Tank Corps. And they saw their share of action:

> Just as the cars were turning a corner the leading car found that one of the barriers at this corner had not been opened and it had to stop. Instantly two machine-guns opened fire at the car from different directions at ranges of about 15 and 30 yards. In the first burst a large amount of 'splash' came in through the observation slits and wounded the driver, Private Hurman and the second, Private Pashley, and Lance Corporal Ainslie, the gunner, was also hit. All the above were hit in the face and eyes: fortunately no one has lost his sight.
>
> Both cars opened fire and silenced the two machine-guns, but not before Lieutenant Newman had been hit twice in the same arm.
>
> We counted 91 definite and distinct hits on the armoured car, apart from many hits that scored and cut through the wings and woodwork.

Official rearmament began in 1934 although there was little public support despite the apparent threats from Japan and a resurgent Germany. Even so it concentrated minds in political and military circles so that the mechanisation of the cavalry, for instance, got under way at a greater pace. For example, the 9th Lancers, then based at Perham Down, acquired their first vehicles in 1937, which they describe as worn-out Carden-Loyd carriers; they subsequently graduated to light tanks as new ones became available but it is interesting to note that this regiment seems to have reached a high degree of efficiency very quickly because by 1938 they were being

The threat of poison gas was taken very seriously before the Second World War. This poor chap wears his respirator, tank crew helmet and communications harness. But we can see that he is a corporal in the Royal Tank Corps by his stripes, his arm badge and collar dogs. What we can't see of course is his face!

used to test and report on various light-tracked vehicles. On the other hand a glimpse of the typical situation in a British cavalry regiment was revealed by a young German officer who was attached to the 12th Lancers at Tidworth about this time. He is said to have written the following to his masters in Germany:

> Here in Tidworth there are few troops and still less modern material, and I am permitted to see such training as goes on during the week. But on Friday afternoons all ranks disappear. Practically no one is left except myself and the orderly officer, who looks after me. I can only conclude that there is some secret training area where they spend their weekends doing up-to-date training with the latest equipment

It is not often that a regiment identifies itself so precisely on its vehicles but this machine-gun carrier, seen in a pre-war postcard, clearly belongs to 2nd Battalion, the Cheshire Regiment. Unfortunately they were infantry but it just goes to show that not everyone in an armoured vehicle was necessarily a 'tankie'.

In fact the Friday ritual remains the same in the British Army today. It is called POETS day: Piss Off Early Tomorrow's Saturday.

As war drew nearer there were some last-minute additions. In April 1937 a new 7th (Army) Battalion was formed at Catterick, whereupon the 4th moved to Farnborough and in March 1938 the 8th (Army) Battalion was created at Perham Down. In both cases there was much looking back to the glory days of the First World War but now a new danger threatened and it was time to look forwards.

Resources

Records for ancestors serving in tanks between the First and Second World Wars are not as easy to find as for those serving during the wars, but nevertheless there are certain sources that are worth looking at.

Tank Museum Archive and Reference Library

Inter-War Ledgers

These are a collection of army enlistment and transfer ledgers (Army Book 358). The ledgers contain basic details of regular soldiers enlisting or transferring into the Machine Gun Corps, Tank Corps, Royal Tank Corps, cavalry and yeomanry, between 1919 and the 1930s; they do not include officers. The army numbers are as follows:

Machine Gun Corps	7807001 to 7868000
Royal Tank Corps	7868001 to 7891868
Royal Tank Regiment	7891869 to 8230000
Royal Armoured Corps	558471 to 558761
Cavalry	309001 to 721000

Many numbers were also changed during this period, so some degree of caution should be applied.

There is an index of surnames for each volume. The ledgers are unwieldy and fragile, so it is hoped to get them scanned at some time. Meanwhile a database of the names is being constructed. The earlier volumes contain a wealth of information in addition to name, rank and number, including place of birth, trade, wife, children, campaigns, wounds, medals, etc., but the later volumes stick to basic information.

Personal Papers

Personal papers vary in content but for the inter-war period they give, at the very least, an insight into how things were at the time. A selection from the Tank Museum Archive is listed below:

'With the Armoured Cars in Iraq and N.W. Persia' by Captain Robert P. Rogers is a personal account, in a loose-leaf typed folder (258 pages), of Captain Rogers's service with 1st Armoured Car Company. It covers the period from the inception to disbandment of the 1st Armoured Car Company. (TM E1991.137.2)

A visitors book, also from 1st Armoured Car Company, which lists names, addresses and regiments of visitors to the Officers' Mess, 1st Armoured Car Company, India 1929–1936. (TM E2008.1217)

A comprehensive collection of service documents for William Steggles, MM, who served for twenty-five years in the army, 1914–1939, and rose to WOII RQMS. The documents include attestation certificate, pay book, certificate of service, warrant officer's warrant, educational certificates and concert party programmes, etc. His service included 10th Armoured Car Company, 7th Armoured Car Company and 5th Battalion, Royal Tank Corps. (TM E1992.124)

A collection of licences – military motor vehicle drivers' licence and orders, a driving licence (licence to drive motor vehicles throughout British India) 1934/1935 and a Punjab Government shooting licence, for Sergeant H. Alley of 9th Armoured Car Company. (TM E1982.40.6.4)

Mechanical and technical training were very important and this is reflected in many of the documents. Lance Corporal J.J. Green of 5th Battalion, Royal Tank Corps, on a course at Central Schools, provides a notebook, hand drawn, on the Rolls-Royce armoured car. The instructor has written 'An excellent notebook. Very clear and neat diagrams.' (TM E2008.554.1.1)

Operational Diaries

As this was officially a period of peace, although peace-keeping duties were being carried out in various places, the Operational Diaries for the inter-war period are known as Historical Records. The National Archives and the Tank Museum hold copies of these records for the Royal Tank Corps battalions (1st Battalion to 7th Battalion) from 1919 to 1938. As with other records some are more comprehensive than others. The 3rd Battalion particularly lists officers and men on courses, postings, discharges and promotions.

The other set of Historical Records belongs to the armoured car companies (1st to the 12th), including the light tank companies. These cover the period 1920 to 1939 and include postings to Ireland, India, Iraq and Egypt. Some of these documents have been transcribed by the Tank Museum and are available for searching in the Archive Reading Room.

Books

Short History of the Royal Tank Corps, **(Gale & Polden Ltd, 1930)**
Two-thirds of this book covers the First World War, but it does go on to cover events in the post-war period. Although containing only short accounts, as the title suggests, it does cover all aspects of the actions of the Royal Tank Corps – including Ireland, Russia, India, Iraq, China, Palestine and Egypt. There is also a useful chart which shows where the battalions were serving between 1916 and 1929. For instance we can tell that the 3rd Armoured Car Company was in Egypt in March 1920.

McInnes, Ian, *The Meritorious Service Medal: The Immediate Awards 1916–1928,* **(Naval & Military Press, 1992, ISBN 0948130 74 1)**
This book alphabetically lists recipients by year and not by regiment.

Other Resources

British Library Oriental and India Office Collections
Many of the Royal Tank Corps units served in India during this period, so the India Office reports are worth looking at. These can be

found at the British Library (Oriental and India Office Records) and can be searched in person, by post (96 Euston Road, London NW1 2DB) or on their website (www.bl.uk).

There is an India Office Family History Search database (http://www.bl.uk/catalogues/iofhs.shtml) holding details of 300,000 births, marriages, deaths and burials, for mainly British and European people in India between 1600–1949.

Royal Tank Corps Journal

The journal covers the period December 1923–1936; see Chapter 2 resource listing for more detail.

Photographs

As we have seen in the previous chapter photographs play an important part in identifying – through their insignia and uniforms – which regiment/battalion an individual served with and within which period. There are many photographic albums for this period held at the Tank Museum Archive showing life in India, both personal and military, with shots of fellow soldiers, landmarks and buildings and vehicles being used. These are a good source of background information and give a genuine feel for the period.

Chapter 4

THE SECOND WORLD WAR

The Royal Armoured Corps came into being on the 4th April 1939, by royal warrant signed by His Majesty King George VI. The convoluted negotiations that brought it into being need not concern us here beyond saying that it was not a happy amalgamation at the time: the social gap alone between the cavalry and what was now to be known as the Royal Tank Regiment – at least the perception of a social gap – was simply too wide.

By this time eighteen out of twenty-two cavalry regiments had been mechanised so they joined with the eight Royal Tank Corps (now Royal Tank Regiment) battalions, the yeomanry armoured car companies (which in November 1938 had expanded to become full armoured regiments) and a couple of oddities which seem to have been added to the Royal Armoured Corps for want of anywhere else to send them. One was the Inns of Court, a territorial regiment with obvious affiliations to the legal profession. It came into the RAC as an armoured car regiment on 1 December 1940, although for the previous two years it had been dedicated to training officers for the cavalry and armoured regiments. The other, the North Irish Horse, was not technically a yeomanry regiment at all – it belonged to a far older volunteer organisation known as the militia, which dated back to 1641. It had been held in suspended animation since 1919 and was now reborn as an armoured car regiment on the same terms as the Territorials in May 1939.

Obviously, because war was deemed to be virtually inevitable from 1938 onwards great efforts had been expended to increase the size of the army, something that in the first place was much easier done with people than with equipment; the supply of tanks was in a desperate state and many of the newly created regiments were lucky if they had one or two obsolete vehicles to train on.

In November 1938 six infantry territorial battalions were converted to tanks and became part of the Royal Tank Corps, but they were not mobilised until the following summer. These were:

7th Battalion, the King's Regiment (Liverpool), became 40th (King's) RTR.
10th Battalion, the Manchester Regiment, became 41st (Oldham) RTR
23rd Battalion, the London Regiment, became 42nd RTR
6th Battalion, the Northumberland Fusiliers, became 43rd RTR
6th Battalion, the Gloucestershire Regiment, became 44th RTR
7th Battalion, the West Yorks Regiment, became 45th (Leeds Rifles) RTR

As part of a belated effort to build up its armoured force, so sadly neglected between the wars, the War Office in 1938 ordered the conversion of certain Territorial infantry battalions into armoured units. One of those earmarked for conversion was a Bristol battalion, the 6th Glosters, which had a fine record and had served with distinction in the First World War. This loss of identity was a sad blow for the 6th Glosters, but with good spirit a high proportion of their officers and men transferred to the tank unit and took up the new role with enthusiasm. This was the beginning of the 44th Battalion, Royal Tank Regiment.

Meanwhile in April six more were created from the original six, these being:

46th (Liverpool Welsh) RTR from Liverpool.
47th (Oldham) RTR from Oldham.
48th RTR from London
49th RTR from Newcastle
50th RTR from Bristol
51st RTR from Leeds

In exactly the same way seven of the original eight yeomanry regiments that had become armoured car companies in 1920 now became independent regiments in their own right with no further affiliation to the Royal Tank Regiment and each also created a second regiment. The exception was the 2nd County of London Yeomanry, the Westminster Dragoons, which retained its RTR affiliation, did not duplicate itself and spent the early months of the war as 102 Officer Cadet Training Unit, before becoming a fully fledged armoured regiment in November 1940. The other oddity was the East Riding Yeomanry whose second regiment became infantry, a battalion of the Green Howards with nothing to do with the Royal Armoured Corps at all.

> So we went happily on until June, 1938, when we were first told to be prepared to expand and to accept up to 400, and then 800 men in the Regiment, and later to double ourselves again and become two regiments. This was the beginning of the 2nd Derbyshire Yeomanry . . .
>
> Ian Walker, 1st Derbyshire Yeomanry

Further yeomanry regiments joined the RAC in the summer of 1939, fifteen in all, of which just five, the Royal Wiltshire Yeomanry, the Warwickshire Yeomanry, the Yorkshire Hussars, the Nottingham-shire (Sherwood Rangers) Yeomanry and the Staffordshire Yeomanry remained with the Royal Armoured Corps. The remainder converted to other arms, mostly Royal Artillery, three to signals and one to an infantry motor battalion.

In April 1939 the introduction of conscription swelled the ranks by some 35,000 militiamen, some of whom would have joined Royal Armoured Corps regiments, but when war was declared in September the call-up was extended to include all males between the ages of 18 and 41 – even though by no means all put on uniform at once, it is said that in terms of manpower the British Army grew threefold almost overnight. There was no shortage of men but they had to be trained and equipped, and those who had been drafted into armoured regiments needed tanks or armoured cars.

In fact expansion was going on in all directions. The Royal Tank Regiment raised four more battalions (9th to 12th) between 1939 and 1941 while six new cavalry regiments were also raised about the

The badge of the 25th Dragoons, one of the six Royal Armoured Corps cavalry regiments raised during the war and disbanded straight afterwards.

same time: 22nd Dragoons, 23rd Hussars, 24th Lancers, 25th Dragoons, 26th Hussars and 27th Lancers.

In most instances these had some sort of affiliation to an existing cavalry regiment; for example, the 23rd Hussars, which was officially raised on 1 December 1940, began with a small cadre of officers and NCOs from 10th Royal Hussars and the 15th/19th Royal Hussars. The regimental history lists most of these men but of the main body says: 'the Regiment was to be largely made up not of experienced soldiers, not even recently trained recruits, but of civilians drawn haphazardly from all walks of life and from every corner of the British Isles.' Not that this was any sort of sinecure. The 24th Lancers, a Sherman regiment in 8th Armoured Brigade, after years of training in Britain was disbanded within two months of landing in France in 1944 to provide trained men for other regiments.

A man might be wearing his 24th Lancers cap badge one day and find himself in a totally different Royal Armoured Corps regiment a few days later. Such are the fortunes of war.

Meanwhile, of course, there was a war on and elements of the Royal Armoured Corps had been involved in the fighting in France in the summer of 1940. These fell roughly into three groups: seven regiments; some regular cavalry; and some yeomanry were divisional cavalry regiments equipped with light tanks and carriers and attached to the infantry divisions. There was also one armoured car regiment, the 12th Lancers, in a similar role. Then there were two battalions of the Royal Tank Regiment (4th and 7th) forming 1st Army Tank Brigade and finally 1st Armoured Division, which comprised six armoured regiments, three cavalry and three RTRs.

The divisional cavalry was in action from the start of the German invasion but proved to be ill-equipped to deal with the German panzers. The two battalions of 1st Army Tank Brigade, assisted by the 12th Lancers, made an impressive, if ultimately futile, attack at Arras in May 1940 which briefly upset the German advance but at considerable cost. The 1st Armoured Division landed in western France and was seen as a powerful force of some 300 tanks that would halt the subsequent German advance after the Dunkirk evacuation. It was not helped by the fact that, in order to relieve the pressure on Dunkirk one regiment, 3rd RTR, was diverted to Calais and effectively wiped out there. The fact was the Germans were on a roll and there was no stopping them. As they sped west the rest of 1st Armoured Division did its best to stop them but never got the chance to act as an entity. Regiments were thrown into action piecemeal and virtually swept away by the onrush.

> My principal memories of that journey are of the heat and dust, and of the thousands of refugees, their faces set in dogged sadness. Of course there were military vehicles going the same way as ourselves, some in convoys and some on their own; but prevailing memory is of the refugees. It was heart rending to see them. This had been going on for days. They came in crowds, congesting the roads with every conceivable kind of

conveyance – battered motor cars dangerously overloaded, horse-drawn carts with belongings piled high and children on top, wheel-barrows, even perambulators.

David Erskine, 5th Royal Tank Regiment, France 1940

Things were changing fast and in this period, in particular, terminology becomes important, if rather confusing. Strictly speaking, at least until the end of the Second World War individual RTR units were described as battalions. Those that operated infantry tanks, such as 4th and 7th RTR in France, retained the old infantry-related terminology and described their subunits as companies, just as they had done in the First World War. In the cavalry they were used to the term regiment and their subdivisions were squadrons

Survivors from 5th Battalion, Royal Tank Regiment relax on the dockside at Plymouth after their return from France in the summer of 1940. Note that the chap in the foreground has a French steel helmet on his shoulder.

Sergeant Ron Huggins and one of his crew loading two-pounder ammunition into their Covenanter tank. Ron served with the 10th Hussars and survived the carnage in France. After a short spell in Britain the regiment went out to the Middle East.

and those RTR battalions operating cruiser tanks alongside the cavalry also tended to adopt their terminology.

In the same way an ordinary soldier was a trooper in the cavalry but a private in the Royal Tank Regiment and there is an interesting commentary on this in the history of the 5th Royal Inniskilling Dragoon Guards (popularly known as the 'Skins') They had been in the process of converting from horses to light tanks in 1938 when this was interrupted by the need to send a motorised squadron to Palestine and naturally it was the trained men and the motor vehicles that went. In an effort to make up numbers in the early months of the war they not only acquired men from their own reserve – that is, soldiers who had served with the colours and returned to civilian life with the proviso that, if required within a certain period, they were obliged to return to the regiment – they also took in numbers of conscripts that would later be known as National Servicemen and some fifty experienced reservists who had done their original service with the Royal Tank Corps. These men were just the kind of material the regiment needed but there were

Men of the 4th/7th Dragoon Guards with their Crusader tank. Presumably on an exercise in the Andover area, reading about themselves in the Andover Post.

problems. The RTC men did not like being addressed as 'trooper' nor did they like wearing the field service cap instead of a beret but these things were gradually ironed out. In fact this is a classic example of the British regimental system: the fact that men felt a far stronger bond to their old regiment than to the Royal Armoured Corps in general, or indeed the British Army as a whole. However, it usually manifested itself in complaints about what we might regard as trivial things and before long such men, if they had not forgotten their first loyalty, now accepted their new role as 'skins' and proved to be excellent soldiers.

Before examining events in the Western Desert there is one other massive expansion within the Royal Armoured Corps that should be mentioned. In 1941 and 1942 a total of thirty-three more armoured regiments were raised by converting infantry battalions. They were numbered consecutively from 107 and known officially as 107 Regiment, Royal Armoured Corps (107 RAC) and so on. However regimental loyalties die hard and although they adopted the black beret of the 'tankies' they preferred to retain their regimental cap badges. For example 107 RAC was formed from 5th Battalion, the King's Own Regiment (of Lancaster), and wore that badge. Most unusual of all in this group was probably 161 RAC. Formed from 12th Battalion, the Green Howards, at Thirsk in November 1941 it converted from tanks to armoured cars at Scarborough in July 1942. Then in September 1943, now at Trowbridge, it converted to become 161 Reconnaissance Regiment but even then it never went overseas but seems to have supplied men to other regiments, notably 43rd Recce which took an entire squadron.

As far as conversion was concerned the story of these battalions is similar to that of the 6th Gloucestershire Regiment mentioned above. Here 9th Battalion, the Gordon Highlanders, recount their rebirth as 116 Regiment, RAC and present a case that would probably hold for all. The battalion had just arrived in India in July 1942.

On the 27th, after they had settled down in cantonments, Lieutenant Colonel Blackater made the fateful announcement: the 9th Gordon Highlanders were to become the 116th Regiment (Gordon Highlanders) Royal Armoured Corps.

This news was received with 'very mixed feelings' but

These men are Royal Armoured Corps, learning their trade in the skeletal hull of an A27 Cruiser tank. The two on the left are Royal Tank Regiment; in the front alongside the driver is a 17th/21st Lancer and behind him someone with a Royal Armoured Corps badge. The sergeant major instructor at the rear may also be RTR.

although a small number of men, regarded as 'unmechanisable', were suffered to depart, the great majority were soon convinced that Gordons could fight as well in tanks as on foot; and the new title showed that their identity would be preserved. Although Gordon Highlanders became 'troopers' the pipe band continued to flourish and every effort was made to procure tartan flashes for all ranks.

Wilfred Miles, The Gordon Highlanders, 1919–1945

As noted above four senior cavalry regiments escaped mechanisation: the Life Guards, the Royal Horse Guards (the Blues), the Royal Dragoons (1st Dragoons) and the Royal Scots Greys (2nd Dragoons). This was regarded as just and proper at War Office level and the magazine *Punch* published a cartoon congratulating the Greys on resisting mechanisation but the feeling does not seem to have been shared by the regiments concerned. Under pressure from the prime minister conversion took place, which resulted in four armoured car regiments: 1st and 2nd Household Cavalry (both composite regiments of Life Guards and Blues), the Royals and the Greys, along with four yeomanry regiments which had remained mounted up to this time. For now, at least, the Royal Armoured Corps was complete. Even so there were still some diehards, people who simply could not come to terms with the changes and seemed incapable of managing mechanical vehicles as they did horses. For these, three cavalry training regiments were created, based respectively in Edinburgh, Colchester and Maidstone. In truth they

Although that is a Crusader tank, and those men look like tank soldiers they are in fact part of the Guards Armoured Training Wing photographed in 1943 and they would not regard themselves as Royal Armoured Corps soldiers.

were an anachronism in a modern war and did not last very long.

The Household Cavalry never admitted to having anything more than a loose association with the Royal Armoured Corps although they used the same equipment as RAC regiments and fought alongside them. There was another group in similar circumstances which had nothing whatever to do with the RAC: the seven battalions of the Brigade of Guards that formed 6th Guards Tank Brigade and Guards Armoured Division. There was strong feeling against putting these men in armour but not for the same reasons of emotion and tradition that affected the conversion of the cavalry; rather the view in this case was that the Guards, with what appeared to be a monolithic approach to discipline and drill, allied to a perceived suppression of individual initiative, were not suited to the more relaxed style of the Royal Armoured Corps, the workmanlike approach of the RTR and the carefree attitude of the cavalry. In the event, as their records prove, they did an excellent job. However, they were not part of the Royal Armoured Corps and fall outside the scope of this book, despite being in tanks.

Since it is patently impossible to cover all the regiments of the Royal Armoured Corps in wartime, never mind the hundreds of ancillary units of greater or lesser longevity, it seems sensible to select specific formations that most people would have heard of and follow them in more detail for the examples they can offer. An obvious one, with the Middle East in mind, would be the renowned 7th Armoured Division: Churchill's 'dear Desert Rats'.

The term 'Desert Rat' is now commonly applied to all elements of the Eighth Army that fought in North Africa, indeed virtually any regiment that served there at all. But in reality it should only apply to those who wore the emblem of the red desert rat, or jerboa, on their uniforms or vehicles. And those people would belong to any regiment that formed part of the 7th Armoured Division. Our business here is with the armoured regiments although it should be noted that no matter what internal changes took place an armoured division was always more than just tanks. It contained infantry, artillery and all the supporting arms such as Royal Army Service Corps, Royal Army Medical Corps, Royal Signals and so on. Just because a man has a Desert Rat on his shoulder it does not

There are times when information is available on the vehicle itself, albeit in code. Here, for example, we have a Daimler Dingo scout car, obviously in the desert and carrying the markings of 7th Armoured Division, the Desert Rats. However, the key is that number 67. It tells us that this vehicle belongs to the junior armoured regiment of the three that constitute an armoured brigade, and if we consult the Order of Battle we find that in this it is 5th Royal Tank Regiment, and we can also see that the two men in this vehicle are wearing RTR cap badges.

necessarily mean that he served in an armoured regiment; as always it is the cap badge that counts.

The 7th Armoured Division could trace its roots back to the Matruh Mobile Force created in September 1938, through the Mobile Division (Egypt) and Abbassia District of August 1939 to 7th Armoured Division as it became in the summer of 1940. At that time, in common with the other armoured divisions rapidly forming in Britain, it consisted of two armoured brigades, each of three tank regiments and an armoured car regiment for divisional reconnaissance plus, of course, all those other elements mentioned above. Following a royal inspection of 6th Armoured Division, at Lakenheath in Suffolk in September 1941 it was realised what a huge and unwieldy arrangement an armoured division was, so from the

Until 6th Armoured Division paraded for the King at Lakenheath in Suffolk, in September 1942, nobody had seen such a sight before. As a result it was soon decided to remove three regiments, about 150 tanks, from each division to create a more balanced force.

following summer the process began of halving the armoured element by removing one armoured brigade.

In the case of 7th Armoured Division this meant that, by the time of the Battle of El Alamein in October 1942 it had just one armoured brigade, the 22nd, which comprised 4th County of London Yeomanry, 1st RTR and 5th RTR. Of its previous armoured brigades the 4th was now an independent armoured brigade not connected directly with an armoured division. The 7th, which was severely mauled at Sidi Rezegh in November 1941, was transferred to Malaya in January 1942 with just two tank regiments: 7th Hussars and 2nd RTR. The situation out there was changing so fast that they ended up in Burma.

The division went to Italy once the fighting in North Africa was over but in December 1943 it was shipped back to Britain, given new tanks and took part in the campaign in north-west Europe. By this time the organisation of an armoured division had changed again: the armoured car regiment (the 11th Hussars in this case) had been removed to operate at a higher (corps) level on long-range reconnaissance while another tank regiment (in this case the 8th Hussars) joined the division as its divisional reconnaissance regiment, later joined once again by the 11th Hussars in their armoured cars. Other changes were brought about not by official decree but by force of circumstances. At Villers-Bocage, on 13 June 1944 A Squadron, 4th County of London Yeomanry, was effectively wiped out by a handful of Tiger tanks and as a result the regiment was removed from the division and amalgamated with its sister regiment, 3rd County of London Yeomanry, which, as 3rd/4th CLY, became part of the independent 4th Armoured Brigade. Meanwhile 5th Royal Inniskilling Dragoon Guards replaced 4th CLY in 22nd Armoured Brigade. Such were the changes that would affect an armoured division, and its component regiments, throughout its life.

For a flavour of tank combat in the desert the following is part of an account by Trooper Arthur Badger, 40th Royal Tank Regiment, 23rd Armoured Brigade (and therefore not a Desert Rat):

> Orders were: tanks would advance 11 hundred yards to a ridge through a minefield which had been cleared and marker posts put up for tanks to move through.

Sometimes it is almost a matter of too much information. The column of Shermans, headed by a Firefly are the tanks of B Squadron, 4th/7th Dragoon Guards on the road between Nijmegen and Cleve in February 1945. The tanks are swamped by soldiers of the 214th Independent Infantry Brigade but you can make out a few crew members, in their berets, on the leading tank. Just to confuse the issue a column of carriers, towing anti-tank guns, part of an unidentified infantry regiment, is passing the other way, on the left.

But Jerry had moved them in the night. At last A Squadron was ordered forward with Valentines and Matildas. The tank I was in was a Matilda with a crew of four. We had high explosive and smoke shells on board.

Orders came through on the wireless to cover the squadron

with smoke for they were being put out of action by mines and gunfire. Our tank was hit on the rim of the turret. The wireless was on fire. The hatch had jammed, Driver Bill Vought was trapped in his seat.

Captain Williams yelled 'abandon tank'. We pulled a crow-bar off the side of the tank and freed our driver. We all dived down and laid flat on the ground for small arms fire was all around us. Captain Williams said 'Who's got a white handkerchief?' Some rude words were said.

Western Desert, 22nd July 1942

Generally speaking British tanks did not enjoy a particularly good reputation during the war. In respect of quantity and reliability they compared badly with tanks produced in the United States, while in terms of armour protection and firepower they came a very poor second to many of the German tanks that they had to deal with. Of course they were not that bad, but the fact is that the troops believed they were, and that was probably the key factor.

Great Britain has often been pilloried for the practice of producing three basic classes of tank: light tanks for reconnaissance, fast but thinly armoured cruiser tanks to range far and wide across the battlefield, and heavy, slow, but well-armoured infantry tanks for direct assault on enemy defences – tanks that could absorb the punishment from anti-tank guns as they advanced in support of the infantry. In fact most nations produced light, medium and heavy tanks to fulfil these different roles although they were perhaps less rigid in their use than the British were. The truth is that the way tanks are handled is the most important factor and as often as not quantity and reliability probably count as much as powerful guns and thick armour, if not more. This, at least, is the big picture but it does not help the unfortunate individuals in a particular tank which they know is inferior to the huge German tank they are up against.

British light tanks from the early part of the war were relatively fast and reliable, quite well suited to reconnaissance missions, but they were no match for other tanks and, as the war proceeded, they tended to be replaced by even more mobile armoured cars. Later, when American light tanks such as the Stuart entered British service they were deemed to be equivalent in most respects to cruiser tanks and were used as such, until outclassed by enemy tanks whereupon they reverted to the reconnaissance role.

Cruiser tanks were generally less successful. One, the Covenanter, was so bad that it was never issued to fighting regiments and only ever used for training. Even its close cousin, the Crusader, which did see a lot of active service in North Africa, had a poor reputation for reliability and may well have been the main reason why, after the fighting in North Africa ended, a whole year went by when no British regiments went into action in British tanks at all. Fortunately by this time considerable quantities of American tanks were becoming available, notably the M3 Grant and the M4 Sherman, which not only carried more versatile guns than the British machines but also offered far higher standards of reliability.

The biggest problem with most British tanks of the second half of the war was that it took something like two years from the appearance of early production models to produce acceptable fighting tanks that their crews would have faith in – but two years is a long time in war. For example, the British cruiser, the Cromwell, would have been a very promising tank if it had been fit for service in 1942 when it first appeared but it was 1944 before it was considered reliable enough to issue to fighting regiments. By then, of course, it was not really a match for more up-to-date German designs. The same was true of the Churchill infantry tank. It ended the war with a very high reputation but it proved so unreliable in its early years that there was talk, on more than one occasion, of stopping production altogether.

The earlier British infantry tanks, in particular the Matilda and Valentine, were, by contrast, quite reliable although they were left behind in terms of firepower. The Matilda in particular was formidable in its day but by the time the Germans arrived in North Africa it proved to be too slow for the fast-moving battles that Rommel practised and proved vulnerable to the dreaded German 88mm weapon used in the anti-tank role. The Valentine, on the other hand, rather fell between stools. It was faster than the Matilda but not so well armoured and indeed served in some regiments as a cruiser tank until 1943. However, it was a small tank, providing little

This posed shot of a Cromwell tank of 4th County of London Yeomanry, with the portrait of Bairnsfather's 'Old Bill' painted on it, shows Lieutenant Bill Cotton (who has somehow acquired an Iron Cross) and his crew shortly after the battle of Villers-Bocage.

elbow room for its crew and, even though later models carried bigger and better guns by 1944 they were outclassed in most other respects and removed from front-line service.

Tank and indeed armoured vehicle manufacture in the Second

World War was vastly expanded compared with the First World War, although in Britain, at least, arguably not much better organised. It involved a system known as parenting, where one company became the parent for a particular type of tank which was assembled by a consortium of contractors and subcontractors all around the country. Take the Churchill tank, for example. The parent company was Vauxhall Motors who, in addition to building tanks at their own plant, controlled other firms – from Broom & Wade down south in High Wycombe to Babcock and Wilcox of Renfrew in Scotland and even Harland and Wolff in Belfast. What this meant was that tanks, or parts of tanks were constantly being moved around the country, by road or rail, until they were finally assembled.

The optimum number of men in a tank was five: the commander, gunner and loader in the turret, plus the driver and a hull machine-gunner in the front of the hull. However, there were variations. Those tanks without a hull machine gun – the Covenanter, some versions of the Crusader and the Matilda, for example – managed with four men, as did the American Stuart, which had a hull machine-gunner but no loader. Most Valentines had a crew of three, two in the turret and a driver whereas others such as the Cruiser Mark I (A9) or the American M3 Grant carried six. This played havoc with regimental organisation, especially when a regiment took over new tanks, and is another reason why men might be added to a regiment or even taken away depending on the tanks they had.

Reference was made earlier to the many additional units that formed the Royal Armoured Corps during the war years; there are far too many to list, never mind explain, and all we can hope to do here is to mention some of the less obscure ones to which men might have been sent during their period with the RAC. There were, for example, thirty-five delivery squadrons, mostly styled field delivery squadrons, although some were armoured DSs, corps DSs and tank DSs at different times. As the title implies they supplied replacement tanks, and often crews, to operational units in the field. This was another way by which a man might come in to a particular regiment. Then there were training regiments – at least nine of these. They would have a small staff of instructors but hundreds of men would pass through them before joining a regiment.

For a while, from June 1940 until early 1941, RAC personnel also provided the manpower for a number of armoured trains in the United Kingdom. Most unusual of all were the dummy tank regiments, employed particularly in the desert, which were difficult to detect from aerial observation.

Whole Orders of Battle were created to accommodate these near-mythical regiments – for example, in the weeks before Alamein – a completely fictional 74th Armoured Brigade was created, composed of the equally fictitious 39th, 118th and 124th Royal Tank Regiments. They drove around in lorries disguised as tanks, usually with a Royal Army Service Corps driver and a Royal Tank Regiment commander but nobody ever belonged to these regiments: in the real world they did not exist and men were only attached to them from their real regiments for a limited period of time. Such a posting rarely appears on a man's service record.

There was one other major accretion to the RAC which, although it was formed in January 1941, was not embodied into the Royal Armoured Corps until January 1944. This was the Reconnaissance Corps, which was created to provide reconnaissance services for the infantry and in most cases operated in armoured vehicles. Theoretically the idea of a corps within a corps was impossible but since it did not impinge upon the activities of the rest of the RAC, it seems to have been tolerated in this case. The Reconnaissance Corps always regarded itself as being something of an elite force, which, at its height, included some twenty-eight regiments, although their period of service as part of the RAC only lasted from January 1944 until the end of the war in most cases.

Another source of confusion that we encounter regularly concerns those branches of the army which also operated tanks, or things that looked like tanks, but had no connection with the Royal Armoured Corps. The Royal Artillery is a good example. To begin with they were generally equipped with towed guns and wheeled tractors but by 1944 some of their field regiments were equipped with self-propelled guns – most of which were tracked and armoured, but mounted field guns – which fired in support of tanks and other arms although they were not part of them. On the other hand anti-tank regiments of the Royal Artillery operated things that

Among the more unusual duties allocated to some Royal Armoured Corps men was as gunners on armoured trains engaged in home defence in the United Kingdom. There were about a dozen of these trains operating during the war, fitted with six-pounder tank guns from the First World War. The men were drawn from various regiments.

Although in this case we cannot identify the regiment, the word 'reconnaissance' on each man's shoulder tells us that this Humber armoured car is serving with the Reconnaissance Corps. The skill at arms badge on the arm of the sergeant, nearest the camera, shows that he is a machine-gun expert. One small dress distinction to note: the Reconnaissance Corps wore its twisted green and yellow lanyard on the right shoulder unlike most units in the British Army.

not only looked like tanks, such as the American M10 tank destroyer, but even fought like tanks, taking on enemy tanks over open sights. There were differences, though these are hard to explain – in the end, as ever, it comes down to the cap badge that the men wore.

The Royal Engineers and also the Royal Marines are mentioned below but one should also acknowledge the Royal Electrical and Mechanical Engineers. The corps was formed in May 1942, taking over some tasks from the Royal Army Ordnance Corps, Royal Army Service Corps and the Royal Engineers and they also operated tank-like vehicles, primarily what are called armoured recovery vehicles, capable of lifting and towing damaged tanks. They operated intimately with the tanks but were still a corps in their own right, with their own cap badge and specialist ranks.

Another armoured division that became famous during the war was the 79th. There is a connection of sorts with 7th Armoured Division in that both were commanded and trained at different times by Major General P.C.S. Hobart, one of the most formidable soldiers of his age. He will always be associated with the term Hobart's Funnies because for most of its existence this peculiar division operated a range of special-purpose tanks to assist the conventional divisions to overcome specific battlefield obstacles. However, when it was first formed in October 1942 it was a conventional armoured division itself, based around 27th Armoured Brigade (from 9th Armoured Division), which consisted of 4th/7th Dragoon Guards, 13th/18th Hussars and the East Riding Yeomanry.

When it took on its new role, in April 1943, 27th Armoured Brigade took on the role of training and operating on Sherman DD amphibious tanks. In November 1943 it was joined by 30th Armoured Brigade whose three regiments operated Sherman Crab mine-flail tanks. The change in role saw the division stripped of its infantry element and it never had a reconnaissance regiment either. Instead it was effectively all armour but with a strong contingent of armoured engineers in the form of 1st Assault Brigade, Royal Engineers equipped with specially adapted Churchill engineer tanks or AVREs (Armoured Vehicle Royal Engineers). There is no direct RAC connection except that these sapper regiments were intimately involved with RAC regiments in the same division from D-Day onwards and many of their tank drivers were seconded from Royal Armoured Corps regiments, although now wearing the cap badge of the Royal Engineers. In fact, although it has nothing to do with the 79th Armoured Division, the same was true of the drivers who joined the Royal Marine Armoured Support Group. Most of them were ex-Royal Armoured Corps now wearing the cap badge and uniform details of the Royal Marines.

Most regiments managed to support a band although not always with full War Office approval (or funds, at least) but few appear to have left any accounts of their activities. However, this extract, taken from the journal of the 13th/18th Royal Hussars, provides some insight into the activities of their band towards the end of the war:

On 21st May 1944 the band set off for an unknown destination eventually arriving at Petworth where the 13th/18th Royal Hussars were preparing for D-Day. The purpose was to play for a mammoth briefing parade in Petworth Castle grounds where the King was to inspect the 27th Armoured Brigade. Immediately afterwards the camp was sealed off but because of a broadcast engagement the bandsmen were sworn to secrecy and allowed to return to Blackdown. During this era the band was known as the No. 1 OCTU (Officer Cadet Training Unit) RAC until the Bandmaster got permission for the band to resume its identity.

On 15th November 1944 the unit moved to Sandhurst from which base the band continued its various engagements. This was short lived because on 7th January we were transferred to 'no man's land' at Newmarket.

The band sailed from Tilbury on 27th February 1945 arriving at Ostend the following day. We travelled by 3-ton lorries through Gent, Antwerp and Nijmegen to join the 51st Highland Division. Concerts and Parades helped to boost morale in preparation for the Rhine crossing.

We encountered Mr Churchill and General Montgomery at Kleeves (amid ruins) and passed what had been the Siegfried Line. We played in the village hall at Ottersum then continued in convoy with the Division via Beck, Gemt and Eindhoven to Bree. There the town crier went around the town announcing that the band would perform on the Bandstand at 3 p.m. – and what a marvellous reception. We were requested to play in the cinema at night. Concerts continued in the area before moving on to Gelden where we met up with the 13th/18th who were out of the line for a rest. We moved with the regiment to Goch where we were shelled when assembling for an open air concert. With five killed and thirty injured (including our flautist) these were the heaviest casualties suffered by the regiment in one day.

It is interesting to note that the men who formed this band appear to have been full-time musicians since they were operating independently of the regiment for most of the time. In infantry regiments bandsmen often doubled as stretcher bearers on the battlefield but that would not be required in an armoured regiment.

By D-Day 27th Armoured Brigade with its DD tanks had left the division since its specialised role ended once it was ashore, whereas 30th Armoured Brigade, with its mine-sweeping flails, continued to adorn its tanks with the famous bull's head badge in the inverted yellow triangle of 79th Armoured Division, right through to the end of the war against Germany.

New equipment, such as the Churchill Crocodile flame-thrower, Ram Kangaroo personnel carrier and Buffalo amphibian joined the division as the campaign went on – attracting new regiments to the division – but the most secret of all was the Canal Defence Light. This strange device, which used a high-powered arc light to dazzle the enemy, was regarded as so secret that men who joined a CDL regiment were still tight lipped about it over forty years later. There were two tank brigades of these unusual tanks during the war although they saw very little action and the theory behind their design was never really put to the test.

> I arrived at Lowther Camp to find nothing but a mass of huts and not a single tank in sight. It seemed somewhat strange because the tanks had always been conspicuous in my previous camps. The mystery deepened when I bumped into somebody I knew who had arrived a few days beforehand.
> 'Where's the armour?' asked I.
> 'Eh?'
> 'Where's the armour?'
> 'Haven't you sworn the oath?' enquired he.
> 'Oath? – I've just got here!'
> 'Can't talk about it. You'll find out tomorrow,' concluded he.
> Trooper L. Blackie, 43 RTR

Unlike a conventional armoured division the 79th never operated on its own. Rather it loaned out men and equipment to whatever part of 21st Army Group might require it for a particular operation, including, as necessary, other Allied armies. Like many formations that gain an impressive reputation in combat 79th Armoured Division has also attracted a lot of mythology which really needs to be filtered before anyone can arrive at the facts. The following account of Operation Astonia – the attack on Le Havre, 10 December 1944, gives a flavour of it:

> I was a wireless operator in one of the Churchill tanks that took part in the assault on Le Havre . . . Our regiment had recently been refitted, to replace heavy tank and personnel losses around Hill 112, near Caen, and the River Orne bridgehead. So we were back to full strength when the reorganised 34 Tank Brigade came under command of 1 Corps for the assault on Le Havre, then under siege. The tanks of 107 RAC (the King's Own) travelled on their own tracks as we left the harbour west of Falaise, on the long journey to Le Havre . . .
>
> 34 Tank Brigade were supporting 49th (West Riding) Division in the assault from the east and north east (107 RAC with 147 Infantry Brigade; 7 RTR with 56 Infantry Brigade; 9 RTR with 146 Infantry Brigade). 33 Armoured Brigade were supporting 51st (Highland) Division in the assault from the north. 79th Armoured Division were to punch gaps in the outer defences with their breaching teams. These included the flailing Sherman Crab tanks of 22 Dragoons, and the Lothian and Border Horse; the flame-throwing Churchill Crocodile tanks of 141 RAC and the combat engineer vehicles (AVRE) of the Assault Squadrons Royal Engineers, with their bridging equipment and fascines.
>
> I was a crew member in BUZZARD, one of the few tanks in B Squadron still to have the complete crew that landed in Normandy. The others were Sergeant Ellis (tank commander), troopers Joe Whelan (driver), Owen Vaughan (hull gunner) and Taffy Evans (turret gunner). Our Squadron arrived at the assembly area on the high ground to the east of Le Havre, on the afternoon preceding the assault.
>
> Trooper Steve Dyson, 107 RAC

Generally speaking those countries of the old British Empire which took part in the Second World War and raised armoured forces did so in their own right and remained independent of the Royal Armoured Corps; as such they fall outside the scope of this book – however, India was different. It had its own armoured regiments and its own armoured corps, formed in May 1941, but a number of British armoured regiments were stationed there too and were often brigaded with Indian armoured corps regiments. It is a complicated business, involving a range of British regiments and there are even instances, such as 163 RAC, which was created from 13th Battalion, the Sherwood Foresters in India in 1942, while 160 RAC, 9th Battalion, the Royal Sussex Regiment, which went to India as an armoured regiment in 1942, reverted to its old title and became an infantry battalion again in March 1943. Many of these regiments served for some time in Burma but reorganisation was endemic and there really is no answer except to consult the relevant War Diaries and regimental histories.

In Italy, on the other hand, where Great Britain, Canada, India, New Zealand and South Africa all had armoured forces, they were at least kept apart. They may well have fought side by side, as did the Poles and the Americans on occasions, but intermingling was rare and, if it did happen, of a temporary nature. There are, however, two items worth mentioning. Although the remit of 79th Armoured Division did not run in Italy, they had their own version in the shape of 25th Tank Brigade, which later became 25th Armoured Engineer Brigade, operating a similar range of vehicles to those seen in north-west Europe and including Royal Engineers. Another contrast was in respect of the American tracked amphibians known as Buffalos. In north-west Europe these were operated by Royal Armoured Corps and Royal Engineers while in Italy they raised a special regiment of the Royal Army Service Corps for amphibious operations in the north-east of the country so again there is no direct contact with the Royal Armoured Corps. One should also mention that in Italy, probably more than any other theatre, tank regiments sometimes served on foot (or dismounted as a cavalry regiment would say) as infantry where that was more suited to the situation. There was also a tendency to mix different types of tanks in individual regiments (Churchills and Shermans, for example), which never happened in north-west Europe. Towards the end of the war most of the surviving regiments in Italy moved up into Austria while others were diverted to deal with problems caused by the Greek Civil War.

Among the more unusual elements of the Royal Armoured Corps are the three airborne units, two of which operated light tanks carried in gliders during the D-Day landings and the Rhine Crossing. The third was 1st Airborne Reconnaissance Regiment, part of the Reconnaissance Corps which operated with 1st Airborne Division until it came to grief at Arnhem. Its men wore the maroon beret of airborne forces, with the Reconnaissance Corps badge, which made them part of the Royal Armoured Corps.

> The flight across the Channel was perfect – the view was simply magnificent with a vast panorama of ships below us . . . Official instructions were that we should remain inside our tank with safety harness on throughout the flight – but this was a sight I should never see again and far too good to be missed – so I lay on the floor of the Hamilcar nose looking down through the Perspex . . . A crackle on the inter-com as we approached the Normandy coast – getting ready to cast off . . . It was time to scramble into the tank, squeezing through the space between the turret and the roof of the glider. A few moments later there was the familiar dull thump as the tow rope was released and the eerie swishing sound as we rushed earthwards, changing to a fume-laden roar as Johnny started up the engine so that we would be fully warmed up with no risk of stalling the engine, as soon as we hit the ground.
>
> Reverend Leslie Burt, 6th Airborne Reconnaissance Regiment

The RAC also had smaller units with tanks based in places such as Cyprus, Malta and Gibraltar. These were all tank men, some of whom may never have heard a shot fired in anger but whose contribution to victory should be acknowledged nonetheless. Tanks were deployed everywhere, from Madagascar to Palestine and Iraq and of course many never left Britain at all, but they all have a history recorded somewhere.

Towards the end of the war the War Office introduced what they called their Python scheme, which made it a requirement that any man abroad with more than three and a half years' service was to be posted home as soon as possible. The effect this had on regiments still fighting was to remove many of their most experienced officers and men so an alternative 'Leave in Lieu of Python' (or LILOP) was introduced to mitigate the effect. Of course this could mean that a man, returning to his regiment from leave, ran the risk of wounds, or even death. It is worth recording that many men took this option anyway, for the sake of their regiment.

Not that demobilisation meant that the soldier had severed all connection with the military. For a pre-ordained number of days after 'dispersal' as the army called it the man was on furlough leave – normally twenty-eight days. He could wear civilian clothes and even take up a civilian job if he could find one but he remained a soldier as far as the army was concerned. Even after that he was

Many miles from the desert but still Desert Rats. Field Marshal Montgomery and Lieutenant Colonel Pat Hobart inspect the men and tanks of 1st Royal Tank Regiment at their barracks in Berlin in September 1945.

A most unusual photograph from the end of the Second World War: five men are posed together with the tools of their trade for a proposed Royal Armoured Corps memorial. They all wear the one-piece tank suit but, by their cap badges all belong to different regiments apart from the gunner (seated centre right) who is wearing the Royal Armoured Corps badge.

liable to be recalled in the event of a grave national emergency and was considered to be in Class Z of the Army Reserve, if he was not already in the Special Reserve of the Territorial Army.

The man went home in uniform and received his demob suit (or a postal order for 52/6d [£2.62½p]) by mail. He was also entitled to retain his army greatcoat although in due course this had to be handed in to his nearest railway station, for which he would receive £1, which was deducted from his allowance.

Most men seem to have been quick to put their army days behind them and tackle civilian life once again. Few seem to have discussed their experiences, perhaps because they thought their families would not understand. Later on they might join their regimental association in order to keep in touch with old comrades but it was often not until they were in their dotage that they started to talk or write about what they had been through, often for the benefit of a new generation. Sadly by then much had been lost, memory plays tricks and mythology tends to overshadow the truth.

Resources

In 1939 the Royal Tank Corps became the Royal Tank Regiment and amalgamated with most of the mechanised cavalry regiments and many yeomanry regiments to form the Royal Armoured Corps. The extensive list of the regiments forming the Royal Armoured Corps can be found in the Appendix. When searching for your tank ancestor this widens the search considerably and means that although he may have been in 'tanks', he may not have been in the Royal Tank Regiment but in one of the other armoured regiments. Insignia and uniform play an even greater part from this time on for identification purposes, and, as for First World War records, medal information may also help. For the Second World War this can be obtained from:

MOD Medal Office
Building 250 Imjin Barracks
Royal Airforce Innsworth
Gloucester GL3 1HW
Tel:0141 224 3600
www.mod.uk/DefenceInternet/DefenceFor/Veterans

However, this will be subject to the same conditions as service record information (see Introduction).

Documents

Many of the following documents listed below are held in the Tank Museum's Archive and Reference Library, although many of these resources are also available at The National Archives. Although not relevant to every family search, they demonstrate the information that can be obtained from a variety of sources. It should be emphasised that this is a selection of resources and is by no means definitive.

War Diaries

The National Archives holds copies of all the Royal Armoured Corps Regimental War Diaries for the Second World War and the Tank Museum holds the second copies. The National Archives copy may also hold some additional appendices. As with First World War War Diaries, the Tank Museum's copies have been transcribed and are therefore searchable. These cover all Royal Armoured Corps regiments, including the Reconnaissance Corps, the armoured/forward delivery squadrons/regiments; the training regiments and the more unusual Scorpion regiments.

Casualty Cards for Royal Armoured Corps

If your relative was killed during the Second World War and was not an officer, then the casualty cards (Army Form W.3040) are a good source of information. They include name, regiment, rank and number. They also include the name and address of the next of kin, e.g. mother, father or wife. They show the date of birth of the casualty and also any previous medical conditions, e.g. tonsillitis. They also show if the person was originally thought to be 'Missing in Action' or 'POW' (Prisoner of War). Finally the cause of death is recorded with the date.

Although these cards are a mini medical report, they only relate to those who were killed and not to those who were wounded but survived.

This casualty card for Frank Percival Myers shows that he was a trooper (TPR) with the 25th Dragoons, Royal Armoured Corps. He is reported as Wounded in Action (WIA) on 11 February 1944, being changed to Killed in Action (KIA) on 14 February 1944 (reported on 1 March 1944 by Second Echelon, India). This is further altered to Died of Wounds (DOW) on the same date at No. 66 Independent Field Ambulance, Burma. The fact that he died of wounds in a hospital facility would normally help in locating where he was buried, but due to unrest in some areas after the war, and remote locations, this was not always possible. The Commonwealth War Graves Commission gives Trooper Myers's resting place as Taukkyan Cemetery, grave/memorial 4.j.17.

Tracer Cards for Royal Armoured Corps

Tracer cards (Army Form B2671) contain information about the transfers in and out of Royal Armoured Corps regiments for the serving soldier. They include army number, date enlisted, training regiment attended and postings. This information is invaluable as the army number will help when applying to the Army Personnel Centre for their service record. The card will also show when the person served with a particular regiment and thus, from the

The tracer card for Thomas William Tait shows that he transferred from the Border Regiment to the Royal Armoured Corps (RAC) on 3 April 1941. He was posted initially to 59th Training Regiment (TR), then 58th and finally 52nd – the former being based at Tidworth and the latter two at Bovington. He was eventually posted to the 7th Queen's Own Hussars on 18 November 1941. The 7th Hussars were in the Middle East at this time but Tait seems to have gone to B. D. & Sch (Base Depot & School?) in December 1941, which suggests that he never left the United Kingdom.

At the end of the war he is transferred to the Royal Armoured Corps Depot, which is to say Bovington Camp and from there he goes to the Royal Armoured Corps gunnery range at Kirkcudbright in Scotland. Finally he is placed on the Y List, which is probably pre-discharge leave, then placed in the reserves (Z) before finally being discharged altogether from the Territorial Army (TA) in 1954. All operational soldiers were initially sent to a training regiment before being assigned to an operational regiment, but it appears likely that Thomas William Tait was in fact an instructor.

Regimental War Diary, where they were at a given time.

The cards will also indicate whether the person was home or abroad; whether they were injured; when they were discharged or put on the reserve list and occasionally when they were commissioned.

Royal Armoured Corps Aliens Register

The Aliens Register is a list of soldiers who had either a foreign mother or father, or both. The lists are organised by nationality, including Italian, Russian, Polish, French, German and many others. The information includes the name and number of the soldier, his date and place of birth, the nationality of his parents and any transfers to other regiments. (Tank Museum)

Royal Armoured Corps Effects Register

The Effects Register is a record of the return of a soldier's personal effects following his death. It includes the soldier's name, number and rank, his unit, date of death, the effects that are being returned and the date returned to the next of kin. (Tank Museum)

Personal Accounts/ Papers

Personal accounts are a wonderful source of information by people who were actually there, although they do have to be used with caution – like most family stories, memory can play tricks and so they might not be entirely accurate. Many Royal Armoured Corps personal accounts, both typed and electronically recorded, have been transcribed and are in a searchable database in the Tank Museum's Archive Reading Room. Many other accounts will also be available at other Royal Armoured Corps Regimental Museums and online at the BBC's 'WW2 People's War' website, which is an archive of Second World War memories written by the public (www.bbc.co.uk/ww2peopleswar/).

A large amount of personal papers are also stored at museums through donations and a few examples at the Tank Museum are listed below.

A large collection of documents for Captain A.R.V. Stone, 61st Reconnaissance Regiment, including service information, family information, letters and poignantly replies of thanks in response to Captain Stone's letters to relatives of troops killed in action. (TM E2004.3347)

A collection of documents relating to Major E.D. Hollands, 51st Royal Tank Regiment, including a scrapbook and record of service. (TM E2009.2123)

A complete set of letters from Captain E. Daniell to his family, sent from various prisoner of war camps. Captain Daniell was captured on 24 May 1940 and released on 29 April 1945 and the letters reflect his feelings and the conditions in the camps during that time. (TM E2002.365)

Examples of Other Official Documents
Record Office Casualty Returns: Prisoner of War Lists 6.3.42–21.6.43 – handwritten ledger of Reconnaissance Corps POWs. (TM E2008.926)

The Royal Armoured Corps Roll of Honour is an original spreadsheet which incorporates the name, number, rank, regiment or corps, place of birth and residence, place of death and date of death. However, the same information can probably be found more easily in the casualty cards. (TM E1975.161)

Medals and Citations
If you are unable to access medal information from the Medal Office, another useful source is The National Archives, which has a file of 'Recommendations for Honours and Awards' (WO373), covering the period 1935–1990, although as the title suggests they are only recommendations and may not have actually been awarded.

Selected books that will be of use if a gallantry medal was awarded are:

Bate, Christopher K. and Smith, Martin G., *For Bravery in the Field: Recipients of the Military Medal 1919–1939, 1939–1945, 1945–1991,* **(Bayonet Publications, 1991, ISBN 1 873996 00 4)**

Brown, George A., *For Distinguished Conduct in the Field: The Register of the Distinguished Conduct Medal 1939–1992,* **(Western Canadian Distributors Ltd, 1993)**

Kamaryc, RM, *The Military Cross Awarded to Officers and Warrant Officers from 1937 to 1993*, (Concept Colour, 1994, ISBN 0 9518638 2 7)

A useful book explaining medals and ribbons is the *Medal Yearbook*, published annually by Token Publishing, which includes information on a wide variety of medals, including the order in which they should be worn. Fundamentally a collector's book, the history and description of medals is excellent.

Lists of medal holders are available at the Tank Museum and many award citations have also been transcribed, although these are mainly for Military Medals (MMs) and Distinguished Conduct Medals (DCMs). Medals donated to museums are usually on display, but unfortunately there is no central register of where medals are and many may be with private collectors.

Obituaries

Many printed obituaries are available from national newspapers, particularly the *Daily Telegraph* and *The Times*, but are also available in regimental journals and in local papers.

Books

The following list of books is again only a selection of the many books that are available concerning regiments, operations and the Second World War in general, although the latter are probably of limited value to the family historian.

Regimental histories of the Royal Armoured Corps regiments are a valuable source of information and the ones written immediately following the war are invaluable. They are too numerous to list here, but many contain detailed accounts of events and most have a Roll of Honour and a record of honours awarded; many also contain lists of officers. Books written at a later date, which includes many of the Royal Tank Regiment histories, are not as valuable a source for family historians.

Forty, George, *British Army Handbook 1939–1945*, (Sutton Publishing, 1998, ISBN 0 7509 1403 3)

A useful book to start off with for an overview of army organisation.

Lindsay, T.M., *Nottinghamshire Sherwood Rangers Yeomanry,* **(Burrup Mathieson & Co Ltd, 1952)**
This is the story of the Sherwood Rangers during the Second World War and includes a Roll of Honour and lists of awards and citations.

Macksey, Major Kenneth, *A History of the Royal Armoured Corps and its Predecessors 1914 to 1975,* **(Newtown Publications, 1983, ISBN 0 950853 60 7))**
This book looks at the history of the Royal Armoured Corps, and includes information about infantry regiment battalions that were converted to regiments of the Royal Armoured Corps in 1941 and 1942.

Miller, Major General Charles, *History of the 13th/18th Royal Hussars (Queen Mary's Own) 1922–1947,* **(Chisman, Bradshaw, 1949)**
As well as detailed information about operations, this book includes not just a list of honours and awards, but full citations for both officers and other ranks. It also includes a list of commanding officers, quartermasters, adjutants, sergeant majors and band-masters. A Roll of Honour is included by area.

Taylor, Jeremy, *This Band of Brothers: A History of the Reconnaissance Corps of the British Army,* **(The White Swan Press, 1947)**
This book lists each Reconnaissance Regiment and from which regiment it was formed, with a synopsis of where it fought. It lists, by regiment, decorations and awards and also those who lost their lives.

Tout, Ken, *A Fine Night for Tanks: The Road to Falaise,* **(Sutton Publishing, 1998, ISBN 0 7509 1730 X)**
Many eye-witness accounts of events in the Second World War have been written and published since the war. They vary in quality and accuracy, but Ken Tout's series of books relating to Normandy, and particularly the Northamptonshire Yeomanry's part in events, are detailed and worth reading.

Army Lists

The *Army List* is an official publication listing all officers, so it is an important source for checking whether a relative served in the army as an officer and if so gives brief details of his career. Unfortunately Royal Armoured Corps entries for the Second World War will not tell you which regiment he served with.

Uniforms and Insignia

The following books may be useful in helping to identify uniforms and insignia, although there are many more:

Edwards, Major T.J., *Regimental Badges*, (Charles Knight, 1974, ISBN 0 85314 214 9)

Davis, Brian L., *British Army Cloth Insignia 1940 to the Present*, (Arms & Armour Press, 1988, ISBN 0 85045 739 4)

Chappell, Mike, *British Battle Insignia (2) 1939–45*, (Osprey Publishing, 1997, ISBN 0 85045 739 4)

Photographs

Photographs of people, as we have seen, are an excellent source for identifying regiments, but photographs of vehicles can also tell us something too. A frequent enquiry is 'What tank was my relative in?' and even 'What was its name?' If the vehicle and the people are together in the shot then the former question can be answered and occasionally the latter. There are, however, thousands of photographs of vehicles and if the regiment is known then at least the vehicles they used can be identified. The Imperial War Museum, which holds all official photographs, should be able to supply photographs of armour within regiments, as can many other specific regimental museums. The Tank Museum can supply photographs of vehicles, but cannot necessarily relate them to a specific regiment.

Royal Armoured Corps Memorial Room at the Tank Museum – Roll of Honour

These ledgers and database include all who have lost their lives whilst in service with the Royal Armoured Corps, from 1939 to the present. This can also be accessed online at www.tankmuseum.org/rollofhonour.

Journals

As explained in previous chapters regimental journals should not be underestimated as a source of information, and below is a selection.

Tank

Published from October 1936 to date. See Chapter Two for more details.

Royal Armoured Corps Journal

From 1946 onwards, the journal incorporated the *Cavalry Journal* and the *Royal Tank Corps Journal*.

Reconnaissance Corps Journal

From 1944 to 1950, the Memorial number of Summer 1950 contains a Roll of Honour.

Eighth Army News

Produced from 1941 to 1945, it was originally printed 'in the field'.

Prisoner of War Records

Online resources for prisoner of war information was given in the Introduction, but there are also relevant records for the Second World War held at The National Archives in the following folders:

Japanese prisoner of war index cards (1942–45) (WO 345)

Liberated prisoner of war interrogation questionnaires 1945–46 (WO 344) – these are arranged by nation, i.e. Germany or Japan

Prisoners of war in British hands 1939–45 (WO 307) – although very few of these survive.

Orders of Battle

Orders of Battle will help in locating where a relative's regiment fitted in the army structure for particular operations and campaigns and thus where they were at any given time (assuming they were with their regiment).

Joslen, H.F., *Orders of Battle: United Kingdom and Colonial Formations and Units in the Second World War 1939–1945*, 2 volumes, (HMSO, 1960) is probably the best source of information.

Another useful source is Mark Bevis's multi-volume *British and Commonwealth Armies (Helion Order of Battle)*, (Helion & Co., 2001), while www.unithistories.com is a website for Order of Battle information. It lists the armoured divisions and includes lists of commanding officers.

Other Museums

Because many of the cavalry and yeomanry regiments have their antecedents prior to the twentieth century, many of them still have their own regimental museums and, like the Tank Museum, many have archives which can be viewed. *A Guide to Military Museums*, (Terence Wise, tenth revised ed., 2001, ISBN 1 85674 035 8) is a useful locator of a military museum, but a list is also available at www.armymuseums. org.uk. A couple of examples are below:

Royal Scots Dragoon Guards
The Castle
Edinburgh EH1 2YT
Tel: 0131 310 5100

The King's Royal Hussars Museum in Winchester
Peninsula Barracks
Winchester
Hampshire SO23 8TS
www.hants.gov.uk/leisure/museum/royalhus

The following museums fall outside of the Royal Armoured Corps but may nevertheless have relevance to 'tank' ancestors.

National Army Museum
Royal Hospital Road
Chelsea
London SW3 4HT
www.national-army-museum.ac.uk

Personal documents of tank related personnel can be found in the National Army Museum archives.

The Imperial War Museum
Imperial War Museum
Lambeth Road
London SE1 6HZ
www.iwm.org.uk

Household Cavalry Museum
Horse Guards
Whitehall
London SW1A 2AX
www.householdcavalry.co.uk
This is the regimental museum for the Guards Regiments, including the Blues and Royals (Royal Horse Guards and 1st Dragoons). However, the archive is still located at Windsor:

Combermere Barracks
Windsor, Berkshire
Tel: 01753 755112

Guards Armoured Division
Guards Museum
Wellington Barracks
Birdcage Walk
London SW1E 6HQ
Tel: 020 7414 3271/3428

Firepower
The Royal Artillery Museum
Royal Arsenal
Woolwich
London SE18 6ST
Tel: 020 8855 7755
www.firepower.org.uk

Royal Engineers Museum
Prince Arthur Road
Gillingham
Kent ME4 4UG
Tel: 01634 406397
www.royalengineers.org.uk

Royal Electrical and Mechanical Engineers (REME)
REME Museum of Technology
Isaac Newton Road
Arborfield
Reading
Berkshire RG2 9NJ
Tel: 0118 976 3375
www.rememuseum.org.uk

Associations

Another possible source of information are the numerous regimental associations, many of which still flourish. Some still hold meetings and have their own journals, which can be retrospectively searched or enquiries can be published in current editions. Unfortunately, with many Second World War veterans ageing, this will gradually become less productive.

In particular, the Royal Tank Regiment Association website (www.royaltankregiment.com) has many links to other sites.

The Tank Museum holds a selection of association journals, including the RTR Association (London Branch) newsletters, the Normandy Veterans Association magazine, the Dunkirk Veterans Association journal and the 52nd Lowland Division Reconnaissance Regiment Old Comrades Association newsletter.

Chapter 5

POST 1945 –
THE NEW WORLD
1945–1960

T he situation at the end of the Second World War mirrored what had happened in 1918 to some extent. Following the defeat of Germany and Japan most conscript soldiers only wanted to shed their uniforms and get home, while the Python scheme further depleted many regiments, not just in the Royal Armoured Corps. Inevitably, of course, in the aftermath of war dozens of new problems sprang up that required military attention and many regiments struggled to find the manpower.

The plan was to reduce the RAC to a peacetime composition of twenty cavalry regiments and eight RTRs by 1947. This, however, was easier said than done because, in addition to occupation forces in Germany – the British Army of the Rhine – forces were needed in Italy, Austria, Greece, the Middle and Far East. Even so, the Reconnaissance Corps was disbanded, as were the various Royal Armoured Corps regiments created from the infantry and the five remaining wartime cavalry regiments. An anonymous example highlights this:

> I started my army engagement of seven years with the colours and five on the reserve on 2 January 1946 when I joined the 90th Primary Training Centre at Ranby Camp, Retford, Nottinghamshire. After my primary training I was posted to 62nd Training Regiment at Catterick from where it was intended that I be sent to the Reconnaissance Corps, but it was disbanded. On 25 July 1946 I joined B Squadron, 4th Queen's

Own Hussars at Opinca in Northern Italy. At this time I was in the Quartermaster and Arms stores so was not involved with AFVs. At that time we were equipped with Sherman tanks, White scout cars and half-tracks. We then moved to Monfalcone near Trieste. Then to Graditscia, where as Lance Corporal I was acting Squadron Quarter Master Sergeant as we were running a transit camp for our troops who were being rushed to the Middle East because of the Palestine crisis. Buzz Pierce, our SQMS, was almost time-expired and he was one of those, along with non-regulars, who were sent to Palestine.

The regiment was then reduced to cadre strength; I was one of six men and an officer who travelled by goods train, in a cattle truck, carrying the silver of the officers' and sergeants' messes, the regimental hounds and the tame fox, to Lubeck near Hamburg in March 1947.

The six original Territorial Army regiments, 40th to 45th RTR, were disbanded and reformed by 1947 while the other six disappeared. The same was true of the yeomanry: having shed their duplicate regiments most were reformed as armoured car regiments in the RAC in 1947, including some new additions such as the Scottish Horse and the Cheshire Yeomanry but many of these were destined not to last very long. Of course these were no longer regiments in the wartime sense, just a small permanent staff and one or two vehicles boosted by an influx of soldiers on evenings and weekends and borrowed vehicles for summer camps and exercises.

It was thought that the spirit, forged in war, might carry over into the post-war period and result in a more homogeneous Royal Armoured Corps but in fact the old divisions were as bad as ever. The Royal Armoured Corps badge of a mailed fist surrounded by arrows was rarely seen, except on flags and stationery, and attempts to bring the RTR and the cavalry closer together was continually resisted, at all levels.

One unusual change which came into effect in the early fifties was the transfer of responsibility for self-propelled anti-tank guns from the Royal Artillery to the RAC. However, this type of vehicle was destined to be replaced in a relatively short time by the tank proper.

National Service, in the peacetime sense, began in 1947 although in reality it was a continuation of the wartime conscription programme, except that it was limited to eighteen months, and then lengthened to two years in 1950. After that men did a further four years part time, as territorials. This would have solved the man-power problem in all three services because the men were posted to operational units once they had completed basic training and from then until the end of their service were part and parcel of their regiment or corps.

Of course there were still men who saw the army as a career and decided to pre-empt the call-up by volunteering as a regular. One such, who signed himself 'Busty' explained his situation in a lengthy article which appeared in the regimental journal of 1st The Queen's Dragoon Guards for 2003. Some extracts appear below:

> In early 1946 I was 16 years old. I had worked in a dead end job since leaving school in August 1943 then aged 14. It was at this time I and a couple of friends met an old school friend, who was about a year older than us, on leave from the Army. He was serving with the Royal Armoured Corps and we were very impressed with his black beret. We three were in the Army Cadet Force (badged to The Suffolk Regiment) and wore the terrible khaki 'cowpat' beret. We knew that we would be called up to do our National Service in about a year's time, so after much discussion we decided to pre-empt this by putting our ages up a year and joining as regulars. Therefore one afternoon in March 1946 we presented ourselves at the Recruiting Office. Changing our dates of birth presented no problems. Birth Certificates were not asked for but convincing the Recruiting Officer that we wished to serve in the RAC and not the infantry was more difficult. He was also the adjutant of the Cadet Battalion of the Suffolk Regiment to which we had been badged for two years and were in fact still serving. He seemed to take it as a personal insult that we were not choosing the Suffolk Regiment. He finally agreed and we signed on for five years regular service and seven years reserve . . .

On 2 May 1946 I reported to 90 Primary Training Centre at Ramby Barracks, Retford, Nots. for six weeks primary training which all recruits had to complete before moving on to Corps training as applicable . . .

On 13 June 1946 I was posted to 59th Training Regiment RAC at Barnard Castle where I exchanged the General Service Corps cap badge for that of the RAC. For the next nine months I trained as driver, gunner and wireless operator on Daimler armoured cars and scout cars. On completion of training I was sent to the RAC Wireless School at Bovington to take part in user trials of the No. 29 wireless set which was intended to replace the No. 19 set, but it was never brought into service . . .

For the next three months 'Busty' is shoved around from pillar to post, never sure which regiment he will ultimately end up in. Following a long journey by train across Europe he finds himself at Villach in Austria as part of a draft destined for Italy known to the army as Central Mediterranean Forces – here he will learn his ultimate fate:

On arrival at Villach the daily routine was to parade on the square each morning when the names of those being posted to Regiments were called out. Those not named would be allocated some fatigues to do and then stand down until the next morning parade. The work schedule was very light as manpower was not a problem. After about seven days my name was called and I was told I was posted to The Queen's Bays at Palmanova. This was the first time I had ever heard of them so I had no idea what to expect. The next day we boarded a train to Udine in Italy where we were met by 3 ton vehicles for the journey to Palmanova. On arrival we were allocated to Squadrons, I going to B Squadron. The next morning I was surprised to discover that after nine months training on Armoured Cars I had been posted to a tank regiment equipped with Comet Tanks . . . For myself my main trade was signaller and as tanks and armoured cars had the same 19 set I found no problem other than as loader. There is quite a size difference between 2 pounder and 75mm ammunition.

Admiral of the Fleet Lord Mountbatten of Burma inspecting Royal Armoured Corps junior leaders at Bovington. At the passing out parade the young men know which regiment they will be going to and adopt the relevant headgear and cap badge accordingly – hence the mixture of caps in this line-up.

The Boys' Squadron, Royal Armoured Corps was formed at Bovington in 1952. Lads of fifteen, with suitable educational qualifications, were accepted and trained to serve as tank crew for the Royal Armoured Corps. In fact the concept had its roots in 1920 when boys were enlisted and trained at Bovington as mechanics to make up for the shortage of adult volunteers. However, this only lasted until 1924 when the army opened its own apprentice schools. Of course the real advantage of catching them young was to channel their education not just into the skills of a tank crewman but, by giving them a head start over ordinary recruits, prepare them for greater responsibilities as adult soldiers. Thus, starting in 1956 but officially launched a year later the title was changed and the force enlarged to become the Junior Leaders' Regiment, RAC, still based at Bovington. The JLR also trained military bandsmen and from 1974 included boys, now at the minimum age of 16, wishing to go into the Army Air Corps and the Royal Military Police.

The training course ran for four terms, during which time members of the regiment wore the Royal Armoured Corps badge. However, by the time of their pass off the boys knew which regiment they would be going to and began to wear the relevant cap badge with a quite noticeable degree of self-conscious pride.

Lots of clues in this picture of a Saladin armoured car in Malaya in 1964. It is RTR obviously from the badge on the front but the Chinese Eye above the headlight identifies it clearly as 4th Royal Tank Regiment. However, look at the insignia on the sleeve of the young officer with his foot on the wheel hub: the black cat device of 17th Infantry Division (or British Land Forces Borneo) provides a clue to the location.

In the meantime the Royal Armoured Corps was absorbing new skills which would suit it well in the future. Peace-keeping operations in India, in Palestine and in Malaya proved that armoured cars, rather than tanks, were better suited to this work and that foot patrols – carefully conducted – were even better, particularly where vehicles could not go. This was particularly true of Malaya, where it ran on for twelve years and demanded the attention of six RAC regiments over that period.

It is probably an exaggeration to say that the onset of the Cold War saved a number of RAC regiments, but it certainly helped. As overseas responsibilities diminished increasing numbers of regular regiments were coming home and as the numbers grew so did the solution of disbanding or amalgamating some. In order to avoid this, at least for the short term, some regiments took on a training role while others, with reduced numbers of men, assisted the Territorial Army, giving the men hands-on experience of current tanks and armoured cars. Rather oddly, at the same time, there seemed to be a diminishing interest in specialised armour, to the extent that only one reduced regiment, 7th Royal Tank Regiment, survived to operate all types. However, the increasing threat from the Communist world required a commensurate increase in the number of armoured regiments required in West Germany, in the Middle East and even Hong Kong. On the other hand, as a reflection of the new tension between East and West a Berlin tank squadron was formed, exclusively Royal Tank Regiment, in 1952. It was disbanded in 1965 but subsequently revived to include other RAC regiments.

As far as the RAC was concerned the Korean War began in November 1950 with the arrival of the 8th Hussars and C Squadron, 7th Royal Tank Regiment. The latter was equipped with Churchill Crocodile flame-throwers although they were only ever used as gun tanks but the 8th Hussars had the new Centurions along with reconnaissance elements of Cromwell tanks and Daimler armoured cars. The same equipment remained in theatre for the duration of the war but the regiments changed, almost on an annual basis: 8th Hussars were followed by 5th Inniskilling Dragoon Guards, they handed over to 1st Royal Tank Regiment and, ultimately 5th RTR. In a sense, however, these titles were almost meaningless. Few

En route to Korea in 1953 NCOs of 5th Royal Tank Regiment mingle with their counterparts of the Royal Electrical and Mechanical Engineers on board the troopship. Cap badges and uniform details tell us who is who while the junk rigged ship in the background provides a clue to the location.

regiments had yet rebuilt to full strength so in every case officers and men had to be drafted in from other regiments, even including individuals from Commonwealth regiments. To quote the late Major K.J. Macksey, MC: 'there was not a Regiment in the RAC which was not, at one time or another, represented among the units which fought in Korea.'

There was plenty of action, and casualties, as the short extract from the Korean diary of C Squadron, 7th Royal Tank Regiment shows:

> (Number) 5 Troop had the misfortune to be mortared and shelled from the North bank of the Han by a captured Cromwell which resulted in the wounding of Sergeant Streather and Lance Corporal Dickenson. Sergeant Streather subsequently died and his death was a very great loss to the Squadron. 6 and 7 Troops managed to put in some good shooting across the river and a troop of Centurions joined in to knock out the Cromwell which had made a nuisance of itself during the previous evening.

It was much the same in the Middle East. Two squadrons of Centurions were maintained in the Persian Gulf in support of the oil interest; another squadron, plus a regiment of armoured cars, were stationed in Egypt, where trouble was slowly fermenting, while a squadron of older tanks, Cromwells or Comets, were in Aqaba on standby in case trouble between Arabs and Israelis showed signs of threatening Jordan. The most settled part of the Middle East in those days was Cyrenaica, where a brigade group was located which had sufficient reserves to bolster other areas as required. The first major crisis in this area came in the summer of 1956 when President Nasser of Egypt nationalised the Suez Canal. Britain, France and Israel responded but the Americans kept away and, as far as the British were concerned, Libya announced that they would not permit British forces in Cyrenaica to be used against Egypt. They would have been ideal but, under the circumstances, two regiments from Britain were earmarked instead, along with a troop of amphibians. The former, 1st and 6th RTR, both required reserves to make up numbers while the amphibian troop was a scratch affair from various RAC regiments. In the end only 6th RTR and the amphibian troop took part and the actual fighting was all over in a day.

National Service effectively ended, as far as the government was concerned, in 1957 although it was 1963 before the last National Serviceman was demobbed. Many doubted whether it would be possible to recruit enough volunteers for an all-regular army without it and ideas on how to do this dominated military thinking at quite high levels for a while. As far as the Royal Armoured Corps was concerned the existing system (regulars were still required, even while National Service functioned) seemed to have been quite haphazard, particularly in the cavalry since most regiments had no particular local affiliations – apart from the Royal Tank Regiment, but that was only in an unofficial sort of way.

Major Macksey reports the result of a Gallup Poll, quoted by the commanding officer of the 16th/5th Lancers, who said that of those questioned 46 per cent did not realise that the Royal Armoured Corps included the cavalry and the RTR; 10 per cent believed that the cavalry still went to war on horses and, to Colonel Lunt's horror, 73 per cent had never even heard of his regiment! A small percentage of those who had joined the 16th/5th admitted that they would have preferred to be in the Royal Tank Regiment, where they believed there was a more modern attitude and less insistence on tradition and excessive concentration on embellishment and colourful appearance.

As a result of these findings and in an effort to capitalise on local interest specific recruiting areas were established, usually based in the area where a relevant yeomanry regiment was based. Thus, for example, the 16th/5th was affiliated to the Staffordshire Yeomanry so they drew many of their recruits from that county.

Of course there was already an established recruiting arrangement within the British Army but since the Royal Armoured Corps seemed to attract more recruits than any other branch of the army their own efforts focussed mainly on boosting the attraction of individual regiments without treading on too many sensitive toes. As far as the Royal Tank Regiment was concerned, following the 1960 amalgamations, their areas were allotted as follows:

> 1st RTR: North-West England with affiliation to the combined 40th/41st RTR TA.
>
> 2nd RTR: London and the Home Counties with affiliation to the Westminster Dragoons TA.
>
> 3rd RTR: West Country with affiliation to the combined North Somerset Yeomanry/44th RTR TA.

4th RTR: Scotland with affiliation to the Lowland Yeomanry
5th RTR: Yorkshire with affiliation to the North Somerset
   Yeomanry / 44th RTR TA.

Note that three regions are not catered for: Northern Ireland, Wales and North-East England and yet many men with readily identifiable regional accents from these areas wore the black beret.

Even so government economies could not be avoided and, following dis-cussions that opened up all the old scars between the cavalry and Royal Tank Regiments a reduction was engineered by a process of amalgamation between 1958 and 1960 as follows:

6th, 7th and 8th RTR joined 3rd, 4th and 5th RTR respectively.
The King's Dragoon Guards and the Queen's Bays became the 1st
   Queen's Dragoon Guards in 1959.
3rd Hussars and 7th Hussars became the Queen's Own Hussars
   in 1958.
4th Hussars and 8th Hussars became the Queen's Royal Irish
   Hussars in 1958.
9th Lancers and 12th Lancers became the 9th / 12th Royal Lancers
   in 1960.

Throughout this period the keynote tank had been the Centurion. Tough and simple, it was probably the finest tank in the world in its day and was consequently a considerable export success. What made it so successful was its adaptability: it seemed to be equally at home in arctic winter, desert sands or the tropics as it was in the temperate climate for which it was designed. But more than that it proved possible to improve the tank's armament to match, or indeed overmatch the potential opposition. The final gun, the 105mm which was introduced in 1959, virtually eclipsed the performance of the 120mm heavy-gun tank Conqueror overnight. Unlike the majority of wartime tanks Centurion was designed for a crew of four instead of five. The missing member was the hull machine-gunner who used to sit at the front of the tank, alongside the driver. That position, along with the gun itself, was now deleted.

Other iconic vehicles of this period were the nippy little Ferret

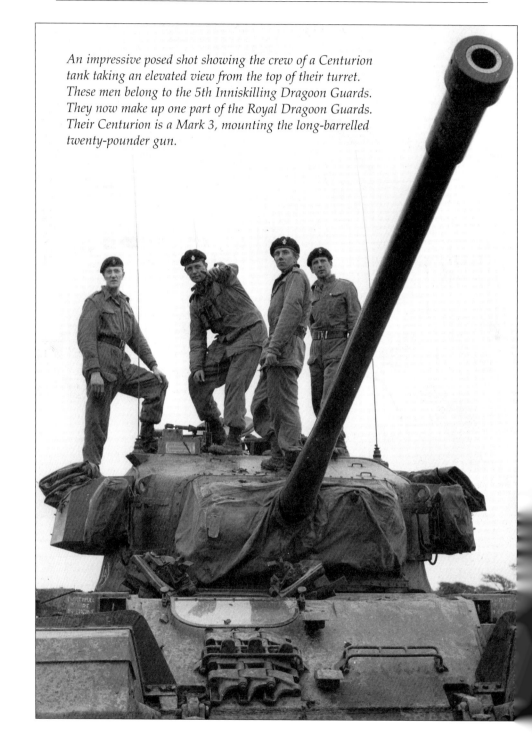

An impressive posed shot showing the crew of a Centurion tank taking an elevated view from the top of their turret. These men belong to the 5th Inniskilling Dragoon Guards. They now make up one part of the Royal Dragoon Guards. Their Centurion is a Mark 3, mounting the long-barrelled twenty-pounder gun.

scout car and the big, and highly effective, Saladin armoured car, although, as we have seen, the British Army was still relying to a greater or lesser extent on late wartime tanks such as the Comet or Churchill.

The following account, by a young officer of the Royal Tank Regiment sheds some light on the demands of peacetime soldiering and is probably typical for many regiments.

> We . . . had been commissioned from Sandhurst about 18 months previously. We had been through two complete training seasons in Germany, having previously done a short Young Officers' Course at Bovvy. We had quickly graduated to be Troop Leaders, starting as operators, then Tank Commanders, and finally taking over a Troop. The quickness of this graduation was due not in any way to our proficiency, but to the shortage of Officers in the Regiment. Anyway, after two training seasons we considered ourselves to be fairly competent Troop Leaders. Our wireless procedure was adequate, with all the current slang; we could do an 857 good enough to bamboozle even the keenest Squadron Leader; we could drive any vehicle; and we had each done a full battle run at Hohne Ranges with moderate success.

Resources

From the post-war period until the present day disbandment and amalgamations of regiments took place, often making a search for a relative even more difficult. When we come to these later periods of research talking to relatives should always be the first step, assuming that they are prepared to talk about their experiences.

The Army Personnel Centre does hold service records up to 1997, but it will only be possible for the individual concerned or their next of kin to gain access to these records. There are, however, other sources that can be used.

Royal Armoured Corps War Diaries for the Korean War and Suez are available at both the The National Archives and the Tank Museum. These include:

8th Hussars Regimental War Diary 1951, Korea

444 Forward Delivery Squadron War Diary 1950–55, Korea

7th Royal Tank Regiment, C Squadron Korean Diary 1950–51,
    which includes a nominal roll, plus their War Diary

1st Royal Tank Regiment War Diary Dec 1952–Nov 1953, Korea

6th Royal Tank Regiment War Diary and Historical Reports for
    Suez

6th Royal Tank Regiment Peace Diary / Historical Reports
    1953–54 and 1958 while serving with the British Army of the
    Rhine

Other documents covering other incidents are also available including the Historical Record of 1st (Berlin) Independent Squadron, RTR, 1951–58.

Quarterly Historical Reports from 1946 to 1950 can be found at The National Archives, e.g. Gibraltar (WO 266), Malta (WO 265) and British Army of the Rhine up to 1967 (WO 267). From 1950 Unit Historical Records can be found at WO 305, documents including honours and awards (WO 32), intelligence reports for 1956 (WO 288) and Orders of Battle (WO 33).

As always, unfortunately, it is often easier to find information about someone who has been killed than for those who survived, so the following memorials should be helpful:

The Armed Forces Memorial website includes a Roll of Honour for post-war casualties: www.veterans-uk/info.

The National Memorial Arboretum
Croxall Road
Alrewas
Staffordshire DE13 7AR
Tel: 01283 792333
www.thenma.org.uk
e-mail info@thenma.org.uk
The names of those who have died since the Second World War are recorded in date and service order, grouped together with colleagues who died in the same incident. There are over 15,000 entries.

The Royal Armoured Corps war memorial at the Tank Museum displays the names of those who have been killed since the end of the Second World War.

Personal Accounts and Documents

Many personal accounts and documents are available at the Tank Museum Archive and Reference Library, including National Service certificates of registration, which will also be available at other Royal Armoured Corps regimental museums (see also Chapter 4).

Journals

Regimental journals as always will have a wealth of information about servicemen:

The 8th Hussars journal, *The Crossbelts 1951/52*, concentrates on events in Korea.

1st Royal Tank Regiment's *The Korean Journal 1952–1953* lists personnel who served in the conflict.

The Tank (See Chapter 2 for details)

The Conqueror for the 1950s relates to the Boys' Squadron before it became the Junior Leaders' Regiment.

Books

A selected list of books is below

Bellis, Malcolm, *British Army Overseas 1945-1970*, (Bellis, 2001, ISBN 0 9529693 2 7) contains Orders of Battle for Far East Asia land forces including Burma, Hong Kong and Malaya; Middle East land forces including Canal Zone, Palestine, Cyprus and Aden; British Army of the Rhine including West Germany, Berlin, Greece and Gibraltar as well as British Army insignia.

Forty, George, *Called Up: A National Service Scrapbook*, (Ian Allen, 1980, ISBN 0 7110 1050 1)

Macksey, Kenneth, *The Tanks: The History of the Royal Tank Regiment 1945–1975*, (Arms & Armour Press, 1979, ISBN 0 85368 293 3)

As well as including a list of honours and awards, there is also a comprehensive chart of RTR organisation and locations.

Gaston, Peter, *Prisoners of War Korea 1950–1953: The British Army*, (London Stamp Exchange, 1976)
Lists men taken prisoner during this period.

Associations
Nearly every regiment will have their own association and these can be accessed through regimental headquarters or regimental museums. They will also be available online as part of a regiment's own website. They are particularly useful for finding comrades of relatives, who may be able to add background to a relative's service.

Chapter 6

OPTIONS FOR CHANGE
1960–1990

D espite covering a long period of time this chapter is only intended as a brief guide to some of the more recent amalgamations that have affected, and to some extent swallowed up, some of the older regiments. The idea being to show how, for example, someone who served with the 13th/18th Hussars during the Second World War would now be catered for by the Light Dragoons, a regiment formed by the amalgamation of the 13th/18th with the 15th/19th Hussars.

However, before we reach that state we need to go back to phase two of the government restructuring plan that came into effect in 1969. Undoubtedly the most remarkable amalgamation of this period was that which created the Blues and Royals – this saw the Royal Horse Guards (the Blues) join with the 1st Dragoons (the Royals) thus creating a binding link between the Household Cavalry and the Royal Armoured Corps. In fact the tendency was to incorporate the 1st Dragoons into the Household troops, with all the ceremonial that implies.

Other changes around this time saw the creation of the Royal Hussars, by the amalgamation of the 10th Hussars with the 11th Hussars, the disbandment of 5th RTR and the creation of the Royal Scots Dragoon Guards by an amalgamation of the Royal Scots Greys with the 3rd Dragoon Guards (the Carabiniers) in 1971. What this meant, apart from the painful loss of identity, was an enlargement of recruiting areas and local associations which regiments had been at pains to build over the previous years.

Starting in 1967 even more drastic cuts changed the nature of what was now known as the Territorial Army and Volunteer Reserve beyond all recognition. In order to survive at all, even as a small group of officers and NCOs, four or five of the old yeomanry regiments combined to form new regiments, either as armoured reconnaissance or home defence regiments within the Royal Armoured Corps. One example will suffice: the Royal Yeomanry Regiment, which incorporated the Royal Wiltshire Yeomanry, Sherwood Rangers, Kent and Sharpshooters, North Irish Horse and the Berkshire and Westminster Dragoons, each of which formed an independent squadron in an effort to retain some vestige of an identity.

That things have changed dramatically since those times is borne out by an anonymous article which appeared in the regimental journal of the Light Dragoons in April 1998. The writer, who hailed from Carlisle, joined up in 1967 at 16 years of age and was enrolled in the junior leaders:

Junior Leaders was duly reached (by steam train from Carlisle to London then London to Bovington, an all-day journey). The first shock, after getting a hair cut (the modern style was to the shoulder which was how I went) was my first proper pay parade, line up in alphabetical order, march in, halt, listen to the pay officer list how much you were getting less all off takes, then salute 'Pay and Pay Book correct sir' march out (£1/10/- of which I got £1, and 10 shillings went to my Post Office savings book). We were issued Battle Dress (BD) as Service Dress (SD) was not quite in, our webbing was black polished 37 Pattern with bright, shiny brasses, sleeping bags had not yet arrived, blankets hairy were still in use. Life at JLR was one round of work, military skills, adventure training and back to the classroom. At the end of the average Junior Leaders time (most joined at 15 and spent two and a half years at JLR, they nearly wouldn't let me in because I was too old) you left with all the formal education to reach WOI, were a full crewman in all tank or recce vehicle trades and could drive a Land-Rover. All that and the fact that you had been brain-washed made you a useful soldier to have in the troop.

Approaching the end of JLR, we all had to go to the kitchen (not the regimental restaurant) where we were told to select which regiment we wanted to join. I didn't have a clue and just went along with what my pals were doing [he actually selected the 15th/19th The King's Royal Hussars]. The biggest shock of all was to discover that I now had to serve my 9 years starting from my 18th birthday. The extra money wasn't up to much and at 16 I had signed my life away to 27, without even knowing what I was getting into.

Two major changes of equipment characterised this period. In armoured regiments Centurion was replaced by Chieftain, the first true main battle tank. Like Centurion it operated with a four-man crew, a driver and three in the turret, but it was a far more heavily armoured tank, mounting a devastating 120mm gun. Unfortunately it also proved to be unreliable, and this through the period that saw it in front-line service. These problems were eventually overcome but by that time newer tanks were appearing to replace it. Various new features about Chieftain grabbed public attention for a while: the fact that, in order to produce a low silhouette, the driver could lie back and drive in a reclining position with his hatch closed; the new ammunition which finally dispensed with the old brass 'cartridge' case in favour of a charge in a fabric bag that consumed itself in the explosive process; and the sleek appearance of the tank caused by the use of castings to create complex shapes at the front of the hull and turret.

The other change involved the reconnaissance regiments, which were now being equipped with a range of fast, lightweight vehicles in the Combat Vehicle Reconnaissance (CVR) series. Once again one particular vehicle – FV101 Scorpion – seemed to gain most attention. This was a three-man tracked vehicle, in effect a light tank, reflecting what could almost be seen as a change of fashion in reconnaissance circles although it was complemented by a wheeled variant known as Fox. Much was made of the fact that these vehicles were built from welded aluminium armour, although that was by no means new, and powered by a Jaguar 4.2-litre petrol engine, which in some respects was a matter of expediency.

A Chieftain of 17th/21st Lancers parked up while its crew takes a break. The absence of markings on vehicles and the lack of dress distinctions means that one has now to rely on the cap badge alone.

Reconnaissance is a skill – some might even say an art form – in itself, quite distinct from the powerful attacking role of the main battle tank, but it became policy within the RAC to change regimental roles at regular intervals. Even so, an armoured regiment would feature a reconnaissance element equipped with Scorpion-type vehicles although reconnaissance regiments did not include main battle tanks.

One thing that has not changed since the tank first appeared in 1916 has been the desire of virtually every man, upon reaching a certain rank, to command his own tank for a period. At all times this ambition was subject to compromise in order that a regiment should survive at all, which is why, while these amalgamations were taking place, some regiments had to settle for what might be seen as subsidiary roles. For example, from 1957 one RAC regiment in Germany provided drivers for infantry armoured personnel carriers, or from 1970 provided personnel for what was then called the RAC Centre Regiment at Bovington. To make up for this, which was a relatively passive function, the same regiment also provided manpower for the squadron in Berlin or as a demonstration squadron for the School of Infantry at Warminster, on Salisbury Plain.

One of the most unusual units to spin off from the Royal Armoured Corps was the Special Reconnaissance Squadron, which was formed in 1962 along Special Air Service lines. Indeed to begin with it relied on the SAS for recruitment and training but since its role was to remain behind enemy lines in the event of a Soviet invasion parachute training was not considered important whereas communications skills were, because the duty of a patrol (of which they planned to have twenty in the squadron) was covert observation and reporting.

In fact the SRS only lasted two years. Many regiments were reluctant to release their best men to an elite unit and were not appeased by the creation, in 1965, of the Parachute Squadron, Royal Armoured Corps – although in terms of purpose this was more aligned to what the RAC was all about. Men from the SRS who escaped recall by their regiments transferred to the new unit, which was created around Cyclops Squadron of 2nd RTR and volunteers from other regiments of the RAC. Equipped at the outset with Humber Hornet/Malkara missile anti-tank vehicles it subsequently operated Ferret scout cars with the Vigilant missile system and ultimately the CVR Scorpion: all types that could be delivered by parachute. Its role was to provide mobile anti-tank support for 16 Parachute Brigade, but in the event much of its activity was on the ground, in the Radfan during the Aden troubles of 1966, in Northern Ireland and as part of the United Nations force in Cyprus. It was disbanded in 1976.

A Mark 2 Ferret stops to talk to a foot patrol in Belfast. The 17th/21st Lancers have obligingly painted their famous cap badge, or motto, on the front of the turret.

In 1968 the most recent bout of Troubles began in Ireland and British involvement in Northern Ireland demanded a stronger and more active military presence. From 1971 various RAC regiments, or parts of regiments, were called upon to play their part, which involved a good deal of time spent on foot in the infantry role, handling infantry weapons and using infantry procedures. It was not the first time that tank soldiers had operated dismounted by any means and it did highlight the inherent versatility of the regular British soldier but it was not a comfortable business, particularly when it involved prison guard duty.

All sections went to Coalisland twice during the tour in rotation. Up the sharp end, under the command of Sergeant

Matthews, the week was a change rather than a rest, as patrolling in Coalisland was infinitely more demanding than Dungannon. Sgt Matthews ran the Ops Room there, tasked patrols, liaised with the Royal Ulster Constabulary, and managed to get to know the local hoods sufficiently well to be able to identify most of them whenever he saw them. Other permanent staff living in the somewhat Spartan accommodation at RUC Coalisland included Lance Corporal Leahy who mended the vehicles, and Private Winson who provided both Army and Police with 'government' food.

Every third week each section was deployed in the country areas which was a welcome change from the town. One notable achievement of the tour occurred when 400 lbs of explosive were found in a culvert on the Ballygawley Road by Troopers Nassau and Bamber, while Sgt Binge found some firing point equipment a couple of hundred yards away. This was one occasion when the frequent task of route and culvert clearance yielded positive results. On other occasions Corporal Hill and a dog succeeded in finding an SKS Simonov rifle and a Garand carbine under a hedge near Coalisland; Tpr Chesham found a .303 rifle with loaded magazine; Tpr Howes spotted a white chink in a gorse bush which turned out to be two fully prepared incendiary cassette bombs in a plastic bag and Sgt Hart in his covert role found a light sensitive device. These finds were not easily earned but involved long hours of searching, re-searching and being told to search again.

Lieutenant Bolton and Corporal Amos lead one of the first OP operations of the tour by spending a very wet night watching a sewage works. VCPs [Vehicle Check Points] were another frequent task. Lance Corporal 'PC' Penfold was not always popular with the local natives with his very thorough searches of their cars and Cpl Marriott came across the Rev. Ian Paisley during one VCP operation. During quiet periods patrols were tasked to do farmers daughter's visits, which apart from satisfying Cpl Dunnage for his patchwork, enabled us to get to know the local people.

Royal Hussars Journal, 1977

The commander and loader of a Challenger tank of the Royal Hussars on the move. A distinctive cap badge is a great aid to accurate identification.

Things continued to change, both in military and in world circles. In order to find more space for training a large area of the Canadian Prairie near Calgary was taken over and by 1972 was established as the British Army Training Unit Suffield (BATUS) but twenty years later, with the demise of the old Soviet Bloc, space was also found in Poland, which probably provided an even more realistic landscape, at least in Cold War terms. And yet, when trouble came it was in a totally new environment where the tanks changed their temperate colour schemes for desert sand and crews learned, as their grandfathers had done, to put up with heat and dust on a grand scale. These locations aside, the options available for foreign service diminished until the only exotic posting, open to a few, is Belize in

Central America, where a few light armoured vehicles have been deployed.

Following parliamentary discussion, starting in 1990 under the catchphrase 'Options for Change' a massive reduction in British armed forces was instituted. By 1994 a series of amalgamations reduced the number of armoured regiments to eleven, although, as ever, all kinds of stratagems were employed in order to subvert some of the effects. For example, plans to amalgamate the Life Guards with the Blues and Royals as the Household Cavalry Regiment went ahead, although by special royal request each half of the new regiment retained its own identity. These also retain men for a ceremonial Household Cavalry Mounted Regiment.

The others were not so fortunate, apart from the Royal Scots Dragoon Guards and the 9th/12th Lancers who retained their identity. For the remainder the results were as follows:

The Royal Hussars and the 14th/20th Hussars became the King's Royal Hussars.

The 13th/18th Hussars and 15th/19th Hussars became the Light Dragoons.

The Queen's Own Hussars and the Queen's Royal Irish Hussars became the Queen's Royal Hussars.

The 16th/5th Lancers and the 17th/21st Lancers became the Queen's Royal Lancers.

The 4th/7th Dragoon Guards and the 5th Inniskilling Dragoon Guards became the Royal Dragoon Guards.

As far as the Royal Tank Regiment was concerned it was slightly more complicated. The amalgamation of 2nd and 3rd RTR created a new 2nd RTR but when 1st and 4th RTR came together in August 1993 there were other sensibilities to consider. Now known as 1st RTR, and sporting the traditional red lanyard, it was agreed to continue the Scottish flavour of the 4th by incorporating the pipes and drums and adopting the Chinese Eye insignia hitherto worn by the 4th. However, this was not quite the end of it. In order to retain two Royal Tank Regiments it was agreed that 1st RTR should amalgamate, on roughly a two-thirds/one-third basis, with 27

A Scimitar of the Light Dragoons attached to IFOR (the NATO multinational Implementation Force) on patrol in Bosnia. Unfortunately these lightweight, high impact helmets, or 'bone domes', invariably lack any form of identification. At times like this one can only rely on dates and locations to establish the presence of a regiment.

Squadron, RAF Regiment to form a Joint Nuclear, Biological, Chemical Regiment for the detection of polluted zones on the battlefield.

Not that this is the end of the story by any means. In an effort to economise yet meet all operational requirements there have been many subsequent changes, usually considered under a title such as 'Strategic Defence Review'. Any effort to strike a balance in one direction is invariably offset by events almost beyond the government's control, such as the two Gulf Wars and of course Afghanistan. This last has seen Royal Armoured Corps soldiers familiarise themselves with a whole range of new vehicles and face up to the fact that armoured vehicles, of one type or another, are now being operated by many other branches of the army. Change is constant but not always in one direction. One thing remains the same: the tank soldier of today is no different to his counterpart of 1916. The technology may have changed but it was always cutting-edge technology in its day. And despite what appears to be a new, homogenous army allegiance to the regiment, identifying with the cap badge is still the strongest bond of all.

Even as the last lines of this book are being written more change is in the air. Full details have not yet been announced but one might anticipate a reduction in the Royal Armoured Corps of two or maybe three regiments. This will be borne as all previous cuts have but it means a further reduction of personnel and by definition families with any first-hand experience of the army and its strange ways, which in turn means that books such as this could be even more useful.

Resources

Information concerning people becomes even more difficult as we get closer to the present day, but regimental journals are always a good source of information as they cover every aspect of regimental life. A few are listed below, but the relevant regimental museum will hold sets of these.

The King's Royal Hussars Regimental Journal (annual)

The Regimental Journal of 1st The Queen's Dragoon Guards (annual)

The Delhi Spearman, the Regimental Journal of the 9th/12th Lancers

5th Inniskilling Dragoon Guards Journal

Conflicts of one sort or another have continued up to the present day but many of the documents and historical records at The National Archives and the Tank Museum are subject to thirty years' closure, so may not be available. So, for example, 5th Royal Tank Regiment, H Squadron's Historical Record for 1966, Borneo, would be available, while records of Northern Ireland and the Gulf War would not. Another example is the RAC officer's lists January 1965–October 1986, which are restricted and covered by data protection for the foreseeable future, but may be useful to future family historians.

Royal Armoured Corps Junior Leaders Regimental Records

Pass out parades, *Conqueror* magazine and media files from 1963 to 1993 are available to purchase on video and CD through the Junior Leaders' Old Boys' Association:

JLR RAC Old Boys' Association
Centurion House
Park Road West
Huddersfield HD4 5RX
www.jlrrac.co.uk

Medals

See medal book list in Chapter 4. A more recent book looking at badges of the later amalgamations within the Royal Armoured Corps is:

Hodges, Lieutenant Colonel Robin, *British Army Badges*, (Privately Published, 2005, ISBN 0 9551463 0 5)

Associations

Associations have continued to flourish and details of them can usually be found on a regiment's own website or through their regimental museum.

Conclusion

Finally, please remember that with any family history research, fact and fiction often need to be separated, as memories and family stories can be suspect, although there is always a kernel of fact in there somewhere which can be built on for the family historian.

Most museums and archives will be happy to help in the search for your ancestor, but unfortunately will probably not have the staff or resources to do the research for you. There may also be a fee and a delay in response time, so please be patient. We often get enquiries from people who think that we have a list of everyone who ever served in tanks (we wish we had), but of course this is not true and sometimes a researcher will have to accept that the resources they need are not available anywhere, for one reason or another. Nevertheless many people do find information about their ancestors, where they were and what they did, and finding this information can be a very interesting and rewarding experience.

Good luck with your search.

APPENDIX

Second World War Royal Armoured Corps Regiments
1st King's Dragoon Guards
The Queen's Bays (2nd Dragoon Guards)
3rd Carabiniers (Prince of Wales's Dragoon Guards)
4th/7th Royal Dragoon Guards
5th Royal Inniskilling Dragoon Guards
1st The Royal Dragoons
The Royal Scots Greys (2nd Dragoons)
3rd The King's Own Hussars
4th Queen's Own Hussars
7th Queen's Own Hussars
8th King's Royal Irish Hussars
9th Queen's Royal Lancers
10th Royal Hussars (Prince of Wales's Own)
11th Hussars (Prince Albert's Own)
12th Royal Lancers (Prince of Wales's Own)
13th/18th Royal Hussars (Queen Mary's Own)
14th/20th King's Hussars
15th 19th King's Royal Hussars
16th/5th The Queen's Royal Lancers
17th/21st Lancers
22nd Dragoons
23rd Hussars
24th Lancers
25th Dragoons
26th Hussars
27th Lancers
North Irish Horse
Royal Wiltshire Yeomanry
Warwickshire Yeomanry
Yorkshire Hussars
Nottinghamshire Yeomanry (Sherwood Rangers)

Staffordshire Yeomanry (Queen's Own Royal Regiment)
1st Derbyshire Yeomanry
2nd Derbyshire Yeomanry
1st Royal Gloucestershire Hussars
2nd Royal Gloucestershire Hussars
1st Lothian and Border Horse
2nd Lothian and Border Horse
1st Fife and Forfar Yeomanry
2nd Fife and Forfar Yeomanry
2nd County of London Yeomanry (Westminster Dragoons)
3rd/4th County of London Yeomanry (Sharpshooters)
1st Northamptonshire Yeomanry
2nd Northamptonshire Yeomanry
1st East Riding Yeomanry
2nd East Riding Yeomanry
Inns of Court Regiment (Devil's Own)
Cheshire Yeomanry
Northumberland Hussars
Leicestershire Yeomanry
Lanarkshire Yeomanry
Duke of Lancaster's Own Yeomanry
Scottish Horse
Ayrshire Yeomanry
Middlesex Yeomanry
Queen's Own Yorkshire Dragoons
North Somerset Yeomanry
1st Royal Tank Regiment
2nd Royal Tank Regiment
3rd Royal Tank Regiment
4th Royal Tank Regiment
5th Royal Tank Regiment
6th Royal Tank Regiment
7th Royal Tank Regiment
8th Royal Tank Regiment
9th Royal Tank Regiment
10th Royal Tank Regiment
11th Royal Tank Regiment

12th Royal Tank Regiment

40th (the King's Battalion) Royal Tank Regiment

41st Royal Tank Regiment

42nd Royal Tank Regiment

43rd Royal Tank Regiment

No. 1 Armoured Regiment (Special) Light Training (Cadre) attached to 43rd RTR

44th Royal Tank Regiment

45th (Leeds Rifles) Royal Tank Regiment

46th Royal Tank Regiment

47th Royal Tank Regiment

48th Royal Tank Regiment

49th Royal Tank Regiment (49 APC Regiment in October 1944)

50th Royal Tank Regiment

51st Royal Tank Regiment

Royal Tank Regiment Deception Regiments: 38, 39, 60, 62, 65, 101, 102, 124

107th Royal Armoured Corps (King's Own Royal Regiment – Lancaster)

108th Royal Armoured Corps (1st/5th Battalion, the Lancashire Fusiliers)

109th Royal Armoured Corps (1st/6th, the Lancashire Fusiliers)

110th Royal Armoured Corps (5th Battalion, the Border Regiment)

111th Royal Armoured Corps (5th Battalion, the Manchester Regiment)

112th Royal Armoured Corps (9th Battalion, the Sherwood Foresters – Nottinghamshire and Derbyshire Regiment)

113th Royal Armoured Corps (2nd/5th Battalion, the West Yorkshire Regiment – The Prince of Wales' Own)

114th Royal Armoured Corps (2nd/6th Battalion, the Duke of Wellington's Regiment – West Riding)

115th Royal Armoured Corps (2nd/7th Battalion, the Duke of Wellington's Regiment – West Riding)

116th Royal Armoured Corps (9th Battalion, the Gordon Highlanders)

141st Royal Armoured Corps (7th Battalion, the Buffs – Royal East Kent Regiment)

142nd Royal Armoured Corps (7th Battalion, the Suffolk Regiment)

143rd Royal Armoured Corps (9th Battalion, the Lancashire Fusiliers)

144th Royal Armoured Corps (8th Battalion, the East Lancashire Regiment)

145th Royal Armoured Corps (8th Battalion, the Duke of Wellington's Regiment – West Riding)

146th Royal Armoured Corps (9th Battalion, the Duke of Wellington's Regiment – West Riding)

147th Royal Armoured Corps (10th Battalion, the Royal Hampshire Regiment)

148th Royal Armoured Corps (9th Battalion, the Loyal Regiment – North Lancashire)

149th Royal Armoured Corps (7th Battalion, the King's Own Yorkshire Light Infantry)

150th Royal Armoured Corps (10th Battalion, the York and Lancaster Regiment)

151st Royal Armoured Corps (10th Battalion, the King's Own Royal Regiment – Lancaster)

152nd Royal Armoured Corps (11th Battalion, the King's Regiment – Liverpool)

153rd Royal Armoured Corps (8th Battalion, the Essex Regiment)

154th Royal Armoured Corps (9th Battalion, the North Staffordshire Regiment – The Prince of Wales's)

155th Royal Armoured Corps (15th Battalion, Durham Light Infantry)

156th Royal Armoured Corps (11th Battalion, Highland Light Infantry – City of Glasgow Regiment)

157th Royal Armoured Corps (9th Battalion, the Royal Hampshire Regiment)

158th Royal Armoured Corps (6th Battalion, South Wales Borderers)

159th Royal Armoured Corps (10th Battalion, the Gloucestershire Regiment)

160th Royal Armoured Corps (9th Battalion, the Royal Sussex Regiment)

162nd Royal Armoured Corps (9th Battalion, the Queen's Own Royal West Kent Regiment)

163rd Royal Armoured Corps (13th Battalion, the Sherwood
  Foresters – Nottinghamshire and Derbyshire Regiment)
1st Scorpion Regiment
400th Independent Scorpion Squadron
401st Independent Scorpion Squadron
200th Armoured Delivery Regiment
201st Armoured Delivery Regiment
1st Armoured Delivery Regiment
2nd Armoured Delivery Regiment
HQ 1st Armoured Replacement Group
HQ 2nd Armoured Replacement Group
1st Armoured Replacement Unit
2nd Armoured Replacement Unit
250th Forward Delivery Squadron
251st Tank Delivery Squadron
254th Corps Delivery Squadron
256th Armoured Delivery Squadron
257th–259th Corps Delivery Squadrons
260th–272nd Forward Delivery Squadrons
273rd–276th and 279th Armoured Delivery Squadrons
277th and 278th Forward Delivery Squadrons
300th, 302nd, 307th, 311th and 312th Tank Delivery Troops
309th and 311th Forward Delivery Squadrons
1st Armoured Brigade, Tank Delivery Troop
K Tank Delivery Troop
E Armoured Delivery Squadron
1st AFV Salvage Detachment
3rd AFV Salvage Detachment
A Maintenance Squadron, Armoured Recovery Group
Canal Battalion, Royal Tank Regiment
K Battalion, Royal Armoured Corps
402nd Overseas Tank Trials Team
403rd Independent Tank Squadron
F Battalion, Royal Tank Regiment
Malta Tanks, Royal Tank Regiment
Gibraltar Tank Squadron
AFV British HQ PAIFORCE

1st Holding Battalion, Royal Armoured Corps
39th Squadron, Royal Armoured Corps
40th Squadron, Royal Armoured Corps
52nd Tank Squadron
73rd Squadron, Royal Armoured Corps
76th Squadron, Royal Armoured Corps
121st Royal Tank Regiment
Protective Squadron, 8th Army HQ
Protective Squadron, 10th Corps HQ
HQ 3rd Armoured Group, Royal Armoured Corps
18th Armoured Group, Royal Armoured Corps School
HQ Royal Armoured Corps, GHQ Home Forces
HQ Eastern Command (Royal Armoured Corps)
HQ 79th Armoured Division (HQ SADE)
102nd and 103rd Officer Cadet Training Unit
1st Armoured Assault Regiment (squadron), Royal Armoured Corps
13th Reserve Regiment
1st, 2nd and 3rd Independent Bridging Troop, Royal Armoured
  Corps
A Assault Regiment, Royal Armoured Corps/Royal Engineers
1st Reconnaissance Regiment
2nd Reconnaissance Regiment
3rd Reconnaissance Regiment
4th Reconnaissance Regiment
5th Reconnaissance Regiment (July–December 1940 as Infantry – 3rd
  Battalion Tower Hamlets Rifles)
15th (Scottish) Reconnaissance Regiment
18th Reconnaissance Regiment
38th Reconnaissance Regiment incorporating 38th, 47th and 55th
  Independent Reconnaissance Companies
42nd Reconnaissance Regiment
43rd (Wessex) Reconnaissance Regiment
44th Reconnaissance Regiment
45th Reconnaissance Regiment
46th Reconnaissance Regiment
49th (West Riding) Reconnaissance Regiment incorporating 24th,
  29th and 148th Independent Reconnaissance Companies

50th Reconnaissance Regiment

51st Reconnaissance Regiment

52nd (Lowland) Reconnaissance Regiment

53rd (Welsh) Reconnaissance Regiment

54th Reconnaissance Regiment

56th Reconnaissance Regiment

59th Reconnaissance Regiment

61st Reconnaissance Regiment

80th Reconnaissance Regiment incorporating 48th, 76th and 77th
Independent Reconnaissance Companies

161st (Green Howards) Reconnaissance Regiment (Originally 161st
Regiment, Royal Armoured Corps)

1st Airborne Reconnaissance Squadron

6th Airborne Reconnaissance Regiment

A Special Service Squadron, Royal Armoured Corps

B Special Service Squadron, Royal Armoured Corps

C Special Services Squadron (Light), Royal armoured Corps

Airborne Light Tank Squadron, Royal Armoured Corps

Nos. 1–3 Armoured Train Groups

Nos. 10–12 Armoured Trains (4th Armoured Train Group)

Army Tank School Middle East (CDL Tank School)

21st Training Regiment

51st–59th Training Regiments

3rd Cavalry Training Regiment

4th Cavalry Training Regiment

6th Cavalry Training Regiment

1st (West Africa) Infantry Brigade Reconnaissance Squadron

2nd (West Africa) Brigade Reconnaissance Squadron

4th Light Scout Car Company

6th Light Scout Car Company

GHQ (Italy) Armoured Car Squadron

INDEX

Royal Scots Dragoon Guards 157, 165

Royal Scots Greys (2nd Dragoons) 105, 157

Royal Tank Regiment (RTR) 1, 4, 5, 47, 48, 95, 97, 100, 101, 106, 116, 141, 142, 147, 150–1, 153, 165

South Wales Borderers 28

Suffolk 143

Tank Corps (Heavy Branch, Machine Gun Corps)

1st/A Company/Battalion 33, 36, 37, 44, 59

2nd/B Company/Battalion 33, 37, 44, 45, 55, 59, 60

3rd/C Company/Battalion 33, 37, 43, 49, 52, 58, 59, 60

4th/D Company/Battalion 33, 37, 44, 59, 60

5th/E Company/Battalion 32, 37, 38, 58, 59, 60

6th/F Company/Battalion 31, 37, 38, 52

7th/G Battalion 38, 45

8th/H Battalion 36, 38, 43, 44, 47, 48, 49, 50

9th/I Battalion 48, 52

10th Battalion 48

11th Battalion 48

12th Battalion 48, 58

13th Battalion 48

14th Battalion 50

15th Battalion 50

16th Battalion 51

17th Battalion 51

18th Battalion 51

19th Battalion 53, 60

20th Battalion 53, 60

21st–26th Battalions 53

5th Armoured Car Company 59

17th (Armoured Car) Battalion 49, 50

Royal Tank Corps

1st (Light) Battalion 80, 84

2nd Battalion 76, 78

3rd Battalion 76, 78, 82

4th Battalion 75, 90

5th Battalion 78

6th Battalion 82, 84, 87

7th (Army) Battalion 90

8th (Army) Battalion 90

1st Armoured Car Company 82

2nd Armoured Car Company 82

3rd Armoured Car Company 82

4th Armoured Car Company 82

5th Armoured Car Company 87

6th Armoured Car Company 82, 87

12th Armoured Car Company 77

Royal Tank Regiment

1st RTR 109, 147, 149, 150, 165

2nd RTR 109, 150, 161, 165

3rd RTR 4, 99, 150, 151, 165

4th RTR 3, 4, 99, 100, 151, 165

5th RTR 100, 109, 147, 151, 157

6th RTR 149, 151

7th RTR 3, 4, 99, 100, 122, 147, 149, 151

8th RTR 151

9th RTR 97, 122

10th RTR 4, 97

11th–12th RTR 97

39th RTR 116

40th RTR (King's) 96, 109, 142, 150

41st RTR (Oldham) 96, 142, 150

42nd RTR 96, 142

43rd RTR 96, 142

44th RTR 96, 142, 150, 151

45th RTR (Leeds Rifles) 96, 142

46th RTR (Liverpool Welsh) 96

47th RTR (Oldham) 96

48th RTR 96

49th RTR 96

50th RTR 96

51st RTR 96